WATER BATH

CANNING AND PRESERVING

THE BIBLE

A Step-By-Step Guide for Beginners On How To Can Fruits, Meats, Vegetables, Jams, And Jellies. Eat Healthier With 1001-day Delicious Easy Recipes And 20 Mouth-Watering Italian Recipes.

TABLE OF CONTENTS

what you find inside!

Introduction

Preserving food is as old as mankind, and at one time every family had a garden where they could grow fresh produce to eat. Preserving food helped ensure that there would be something to eat during the cold winter months. Canning, or preserving foods in cans or jars, is a way of preserving foods.

How Canning Preserves Foods?

Canning is a process of heating food to a prescribed temperature to kill bacteria. Raw foods can be "cooked" or heated in a few different ways including boiling, baking, steaming, and canning. Canning is usually done in jars, and it is important that all jars are clean and sterilized or the food will spoil. Once cans are filled, they need to be sealed to prevent any unsterilized air from seeping into the food. Canning also creates steam inside the can or jar, and pressure builds as this steam rises against a lid or seal. This pressure forces air out of the airspace between the lid and foil liner within a closed can, which keeps it fresh longer.

The Basics of Canning Food

There are several different methods of canning foods. Open canning, when jars of food are placed into boiling water on the stovetop just like any other soup or stew. Water bath canning is another method where the jars are placed in a water bath and boiled at various temperatures depending on what needs to be preserved in them for how long. The third method is pressure canning where food is placed inside a sealed metal container and pressurized to at least 240 degrees Fahrenheit. Pressure canning is used for low-acid foods like vegetables, meats, and seafood because it can expose these foods too much higher temperatures than water bath canning.

Ensuring Safe Canned Foods

In order to make home canning safe, people must use tested recipes that have been proven safe in recent years. It's not just the recipe that matters when it comes to safety. People should also follow all directions and use good, fresh ingredients so that they do not run the risk of getting sick from their canned food.

For Safety's Sake :

The exact times that food is safely canned at home will depend on the recipe and the variety of food being canned. But it is important to take certain precautions when canning foods at home. Always wash and clean your jars before you begin, even if it is just a little bit of soap to get rid of any germs in the jars or lids. The idea here is to keep germs from getting into any food product that goes in those jars because once they are added in there won't be much you can do about them. Take your finished product out of the jar after it has been sealed and refrigerated correctly, so as not to give food pathogens an opportunity for survival.

Equipment and Methods Not Recommended

Some people like to use certain equipment or methods when canning their foods, but experts say these are not recommended.

- Using any kind of vinegar, even if it is a low-acid kind, is not recommended. Vinegar can turn into an acidic substance that will cause other food to spoil after being canned.
- Scientists say that storing foods in the refrigerator is no safer than storing them in a can or jar at room temperature. If you decide to store your food in the refrigerator, remove it from there as soon as it is done so you don't let any dangerous pathogens grow while it gets stored there.
- People should never try to can meats that still have the fat cap on them, and it is not recommended to can chicken pieces that still have the skin on them. This kind of food can become contaminated easily, especially if it is home-canned without using pressure as a method.
- Experts say to never use pressure canning home-canned meats.
- It is important not to overcrowd jars when you fill them with hot food. A rule of thumb is one quart of food fits in a pint jar, so if you have two quarts of food, then you should have four jars filled and sealed.
- Different foods require different temperatures in order to be safe when they are canned. You must use the right temperature for the recipe. The USDA has a handy chart that will take you through the steps exactly, which can be found online at www.nalpreservingfoods.gov/canningfaq/index.html .

Ensuring High-Quality Canned Foods

When it comes to quality in canned foods, it's important not to skimp on the ingredients. Also, it's important to take care of canned foods once they are opened. It is best to use them without being opened for at least six months.

Quality is a personal preference, but experts recommend using a good variety of food when you are canning because that way you will have something safe and fresh-tasting even if some jars aren't perfect, and you can still have some usable food after the lids and bottoms start falling apart.

Avoid using anything that has been previously canned or may have a lot of impurities in the jars or lids when you are canning your own foods.

Recommended Jars and Lids

When you are canning, you want to use jars and lids that work with each other to seal the jars. The lids should fit tightly, and they should be made from a material that is safe for food. The lids do not need to be heat-resistant, but they should be able to withstand temperatures as high as 250 degrees Fahrenheit.

Selecting the right size jar for your canned foods means getting the right amount of food in it and making sure that it will fit well in your jar or canner.

Recommended Canners for Home Canning

There are several different kinds of canners available for use, but the best ones are pressure canners, and they should be chosen carefully in order to get the most out of them.

The pressure canner is not a new invention – it was actually invented in the mid-nineteenth century – and what makes them great is the way they seal jars. The water in the bottom builds up steam, pushing against a spring-loaded lid until the air is driven out and the steam inside is able to increase pressure inside the jar. This means that your food will be cooked evenly.

Selecting the Correct Processing Time

There are several factors to take into account when you are working with canned food at home. Temperature is one of these, but the others are things like altitude, size of jars, type of food being canned, and whether or not it needs to be processed longer than others.

The temperature at which the food was cooked will be different for every recipe. Typically the temperature will be between 240 and 250 degrees Fahrenheit for most recipes.

There is a chart on the USDA website that takes you through how much time you need to add to your canning process depending on what ingredients you use in your recipe and how high up you live.

Cooling Jars and Testing Jar Seals

When you have finished canning your food, it is important to cool the jars off so that they will not rust and contaminate other canned foods. This takes some time, and it is recommended to wait 24 hours before opening the jar. When you open a jar, use your finger to test the inside of the jar. If it seems clean and dry inside, then these jars are safe for use in canning again.

Storing Home Canned Foods

After you have finished canning as much food as you want, it is recommended to store it in the refrigerator and to use it within a month. After that, the food should be disposed of so that someone else won't risk eating spoiled foods.

When it comes to home-canned food, experts recommend sealing the jars in order to keep any contaminants out.

You should wash your jars and lids thoroughly before putting them away so that they are not used for other foods later on.

It's important not to reuse lids unless you intend on canning something with a high quantity of food inside of them again or if all of your jars have become unusable without their lids.

Identifying and Handling Spoiled Canned Food

The most common reasons for spoiled home-canned food are improper handling and poor storage conditions, but the signs of spoilage are easy to identify. Mold will appear on food that was canned improperly or in an unclean jar or canner, such as meats that have been canned without being completely cooked. This means that they were not hot enough to kill the bacteria that causes mold, and more importantly, botulism poisoning.

Canned Foods for Special Diets

Canning food is a great way to ensure that you and your family will have something delicious to eat when you are a little short on time. But canned food can also be used for special diets. For example, if you are diabetic or have certain health issues, then it's important that you make sure that your diet is safe for the condition. The same goes for those with dietary restrictions or allergies – they want to make sure that they get healthy foods into their bodies without having to worry about them being dangerous.

Canning Fruit-based Baby Foods

Fruit-based baby foods are a great way to give your baby all of the healthy foods in the fresh produce that he or she would normally eat. The fruits you want to include can be canned, and the process will ensure that they are safely preserved for your child for many years.

Canned Fruits and Vegetables for Improved Nutrition

Canned food is very nutritious, and it's an easy way to make sure that you're feeding your family healthy meals without having to babysit the process. Canned vegetables can help you provide your family with a variety of vitamins and minerals that will help to keep it healthy.

Temperatures for Food Preservation

Different methods and recipes for preserving food will require certain temperatures before, during, and after the process. It is important to know how high to heat your foods and what temperatures are safe for your family.

Understanding Environmental Stewardship

There are many different methods of preserving food at home, but they all depend on the same thing: ensuring that the quality of the food that you are canning is maintained as it goes through the different steps in the preservation process. The most essential element for making sure this happens is careful monitoring of temperatures inside of jars or cans as they are processed. 6.

Temperatures at which Water Boils at Different Altitudes

In order to preserve food, it is important that you prepare the ingredients properly. In boiling water bath canning, it is important to know the correct temperature for boiling water and how high above sea level that can be achieved.

The Purpose of Fumigation

Food preservation methods like fumigation are used to kill germs in food, as well as insects and other organisms. Fumigation also helps prevent decay in freshly harvested foods prior to processing or preserving them so they are safely eaten by humans or animals.

Causes and Possible Solutions for Problems with Canned Food

If preserved food develops an odor, it doesn't look good, or the seal on the container leaks after opening, then there could be a problem. Those are common problems with canned food that you may need to deal with if you have any of those issues.

Canned Food Storage Time

It is possible to eat canned food after many years in storage, but it isn't necessarily the best tasting thing in the world. Canned foods made at home tend to be used within a few months after they are canned, but commercial products can last for several years if you take care of them properly.

Causes and Possible Solutions for Problems with Canned Fruit Juices

Sometimes canned fruits and fruit juice can develop an off odor, but that's only a small part of the problem. The problem is often one of spoilage. If the fruit doesn't contain enough sugar, as happens with other products, then it will spoil, and that can cause a bad smell. The key to preventing this situation is to store fruits at cool temperatures away from heat (and out of direct sunlight).

While it's possible to find someone who has developed an immunity to botulism, it's not likely. Most people are cautioned about the dangers of botulism poisoning by the USDA for a reason, and that is because they want to ensure that canned food products are safe for everyone.

Canned Fruit Juices

Consuming canned fruit juices on a regular basis can be very beneficial for your health, especially if you have less time to prepare fresh fruit when you are working or living in places where fresh produce isn't readily available.

The Importance of Toxin Removal

Many people feel like they can get away with eating canned foods without worrying about the process that is used to remove toxins from foods before they are canned. The truth is that no food should be consumed unless it has been thoroughly prepared, and toxins need to be removed in order to ensure food safety.

Find Your Altitude

There are several methods for determining the temperature of water at various altitudes. However, it is crucial to know that there is a difference between the boiling point and the freezing point.

The Importance of a Pressure Canner

Pressure canners are the best canners to use when you are preserving food at home. There are many benefits to using pressure canners: they distribute the heat evenly around the jars, they reduce the amount of time it takes to preserve food, and they reduce the risk of botulism poisoning.

When Canning Meat

Meat should be cooked until done, and when canning food, you want to be sure that it is completely cooked in order to avoid spoilage and food poisoning risk. It's also important not to overcook meat in order to keep it safe to eat.

Fruit Syrups

Syrup Type	Approx. % Sugar	Measures of Water and Sugar				Fruits Commonly packed in syrup (2)
		For 9-Pt Load (1)		For 7-Qt Load		
		Cups Water	Cups Sugar	Cups Water	Cups Sugar	
Very Light	10	6-1/2	3/4	10-1/2	1-1/4	Approximates natural sugar levels in most fruits and adds the fewest calories.
Light	20	5-3/4	1-1/2	9	2-1/4	Very sweet fruit. Try a small amount the first time to see if your family likes it.
Medium	30	5-1/4	2-1/4	8-1/4	3-3/4	Sweet apples, sweet cherries, berries, grapes.
Heavy	40	5	3-1/4	7-3/4	5-1/4	Tart apples, apricots, sour cherries, gooseberries, nectarines, peaches, pears, plums.
Very Heavy	50	4-1/4	4-1/4	6-1/2	6-3/4	Very sour fruit. Try a small amount the first time to see if your family likes it.

Chicken or Rabbit

Style of Pack	Jar Size	Process Time	Canner Pressure (PSI) at Altitudes of			
			0- 2,000 ft	2,001 - 4,000 ft	4,001 - 6,000 ft	6,001 - 8,000 ft
Without Bones:						
	Pints	75 min	11 lb	12 lb	13 lb	14 lb
	Quarts	90	11	12	13	14
With Bones:						
	Pints	65 min	11 lb	12 lb	13 lb	14 lb
	Quarts	75	11	12	13	14

Strips, Cubes, or Chunks of Meat

Style of Pack	Jar Size	Process Time	Canner Pressure (PSI) at Altitudes of			
			0 - 2,000 ft	2,001 - 4,000 ft	4,001 - 6,000 ft	6,001 - 8,000 ft
	Pints	75 min	**11 lb**	12 lb	13 lb	14 lb
	Quarts	90	**11**	12	13	14

Fish

Style of Pack	Jar Size	Process Time	Canner Pressure (PSI) at Altitudes of			
			0 - 2,000 ft	2,001 - 4,000 ft	4,001 - 6,000 ft	6,001 - 8,000 ft
Raw	Pints	100 min	**11 lb**	12 lb	13 lb	14 lb

Chapter 1

20 MOUTH-WATERING ITALIAN RECIPES

CHAPTER 1
ITALIAN RECIPES

Tomato Sauce

- 2 kg Ripe tomatoes
- Basil
- Salt (just enough)
- Yield: 1 kg of tomatoes = about

- 35ml of puree
- d shape.

To prepare the tomato puree preserves for the whole year, buy tomatoes that are not bruised, but firm, well red and ripe. You can choose between the coppery cluster and round tomatoes, or the San Marzano, with an elongated shape.

DIRECTIONS

1. To prepare the tomato sauce, start by checking them individually, then remove the rotten, stained, or bruised ones. Remove the stalks and wash them very well. Leave them to drain. Cut each tomato in half and remove the seeds

2. Place them in a large pot and let them dry over low heat by covering them with a lid. Turn them from time to time until they are limp and pulp. At this point, pass them through a vegetable mill (or with a special electric machine), making the sauce converge in a smaller steel pot. In the meantime, you have to sanitize the jars and lids by boiling them in plenty of water or using a special sterilizer.

3. If the tomato puree does not seem to be of the right density, filter it with a little mesh strainer to remove excess water or let it thicken on the stove until it reaches the desired consistency.

4. Put some basil leaves inside each sanitized jar. Pour the tomato puree into the sanitized jars with the help of a funnel and ensure to leave 2-3 cm of space from the edge of the jar. Finish with a few more basil leaves and close the jars well. At this point, proceed with boiling: place the jars inside a large container, and make sure you separate them from each other with clean cotton sheets, add hot water until they are covered, and then boil. Turn off the heat 30 minutes after boiling it and let it cool. Once the jars are cold, check that the vacuum has been done correctly: if, by pressing the cap, you DO NOT hear the "click clack", the vacuum will have formed correctly. Store the tomato puree in a cool place away from light.

5. If the vacuum has been done correctly, the tomato puree can be stored for a maximum of one year in a cool place away from light.

Red Sauce
(WITH PEPPERS)

An excellent and delicious sauce to be used to season boiled meats (hot or cold), roasts or to be eaten spread on toasted bread to accompany cheeses and cold cuts. The recipe is that of my grandmother. I slightly adopted it using industrial tomato paste (the one in a tube, so to speak) to make it slightly lighter. With the homemade concentrate, the sauce was much tastier, but definitely heavy. With the following ingredients, I prepared 8 jars of 100g. Here is the recipe for this delicious pepper sauce.

SHOPPING LIST

- red and yellow peppers
- 1 kg white onions (I use the sweet ones from Giarratana)
- 1 kg green tomatoes
- 600 gr white wine vinegar (I measure it with an old bottle)
- 300 gr sugar
- 300 gr extra virgin olive oil
- 1 double tomato concentrate tube

DIRECTIONS

1. First wash the peppers very well, remove the seeds and the white internal filaments, then cut them into tiny pieces.
2. Wash the tomatoes the same way, remove the seeds inside, and cut them into small cubes. Put everything in a saucepan, make sure you use a flame spreading net even if you are not using (as I do) an earthenware saucepan, add the vinegar, sugar, and oil, and put on the fire.
3. As soon as it starts boiling, cook for 15-20 minutes, then add the entire tube of tomato paste. Mix well using a wooden spoon and leave to cook over low heat for about 3 hours. Half an hour before the three hours, remove from the heat and (this is my variant) with an immersion mixer suitable for blending hot foods, mix everything as well.
4. Finish cooking. At this point, the sauce is ready to be poured into the special pre-sterilized glass jars.
5. Cover the jars and turn them upside down so that the vacuum is created. Let them cool completely covered with a kitchen towel.
6. When they are completely cooled, wrap each jar in a napkin and place them in a pot large enough to contain them all.
7. Cover them with cold water and boil them for 20 minutes. Let them cool completely in the same boiling water, then dry them and store them in a cool, dry place.
8. once opened, the jars should be kept in the refrigerator and the sauce consumed quickly.

Pinuccia Olives

SHOPPING LIST

- 1 kg olives.
- 15 bay leaves.
- 5 dried wild fennel branches.
- salt 3 tablespoons (or to taste).

DIRECTIONS

1. Let each olive absorb the water. Soak in cold water and change it every 1 or 2 days for 15 times.
2. Boil fennel bay leaves and salt in a 5-liter pot for at least 2 hours. Let it cool completely then put the olives in it.
3. Put them in the jar with water to the brim and let them rest for at least 2 days before consuming them. Always make sure that the olives remain covered by water.

8

Carciofini Sott'olio
ARTICHOKES IN OIL

SHOPPING LIST

- artichokes to fill the jar
- extravirgin olive or sunflowers oil
- 20 gr of back pepper grains
- Laurel leaves

DIRECTIONS

1. Boil the artichokes in water and vinegar for 3 minutes after the boiling starts.

2. Drain them and let them dry during the night wrapped up in a towel.
Finally put the artichokes in the jars together with pepper and laurel leaves.

3. Strong pressing the content so as to avoid creating air bubbles.

3. Fill the jar with oil to the brim, and bang the jar on the table to bring up any air bubbles.

4. Do not close the jars immediately, leave the lid on, unscrewed, for at least half a day. Before sealing the jar, check if more oil is needed, the artichokes must be completely immersed in the oil.

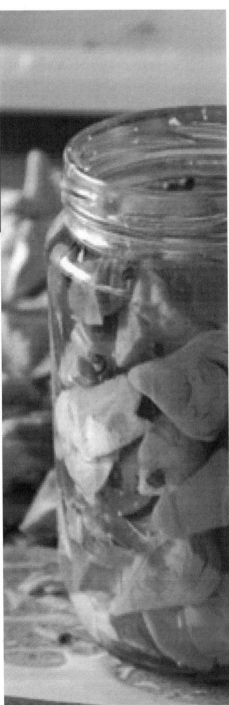

Marmellata Di Fichi

- 1 kg figs
- 1 kg sugar
- 1 untreated lemon (juice and lemon zest)

DIRECTIONS

1. Clean the figs with a damp cloth without peeling them and cut them into quarters.
2. Put them in a saucepan and add the grated lemon peel, then put everything on low heat. Make sure you place a spread-flare net on the stove. Cook until the figs have almost completely spread.
3. Pass the figs to the green pastry (or blend them with an immersion mixer of those suitable to blend hot foods) or if you want a greater consistency of jam avoid this step. I prefer (and recommend) the second solution.
4. Add the sugar and let it mix, stirring constantly and continuously so that the bottom does not caramelize. Cook for 20 to 30 minutes and anyway - until the jam has veiled the spoon.
5. Invade the fig jam in jars already sterilized, filling them to the brim. Close tightly and topple the jars by holding them at the lids so that they create the vacuum.
6. Leave it (covered with a kitchen towel) to cool completely.
7. Finally, wrap the individual jars with napkins and place them in a large pot with high edges. Cover the jars with cold water and boil. Boil for at least 20 minutes. Turn off the heat and let them cool in the same water, then take them out, dry them and place them in a cool, dry, and semi-dark place.
8. Like all jams, it is better to consume it after at least 30 days of its preparation.

Funghi Porcini
SOTT'OLIO

- 1.5g small porcini mushrooms
- 400g extra virgin olive oil
- 1/2 glass dry white wine
- 1/2 cup white wine vinegar
- 1 litre water
- 4 laurel clean bay leaves
- salt (to taste)

DIRECTIONS

1. Clean them very thoroughly with a damp towel trying to eliminate all the soil, and if necessary pass them under cold running water but very quickly and make them dry well.
2. Cut them into slices if they were quite large and remove the skin from the stems otherwise they would turn out to be hard.
3. Boil the water, then add the vinegar, and the white wine, once the boil resumes pour the mushrooms and cook over a moderate flame for 10 minutes, stirring often with a wooden spoon gently, turn off and drain the mushrooms using a clean towel and let them dry perfectly.
4. Put the mushrooms in the previously sterilized pot, seasoned with the bay leaves and peppercorns.
5. Cover with olive oil and leave it for about a week. Refill the oil in case the level in the pot drops.
6. Sterilize the pots by putting them in a pot with cold water. After boiling, count 30 minutes from the boil and leave to cool completely in the pot and place in a dark and cool place.

Tonno
SOTT'OLIO

🛒 SHOPPING LIST

- Dose for 2 jars
- 1 kg of tuna fish
- extravirgin olive oil
- 1 liter of water
- 75 gr of salt
- 6 juniper berries
- 6 bay leaves

▶ DIRECTIONS

1. Wash the tuna repeatedly with cold water until it loses all the blood. Boil the water in a saucepan.
2. Add the bay leaves, salt, and juniper berries.
3. Add it to the pot and cook it over medium heat for about 1 hour.
4. After this time, let it drain in a bowl for 24 hours.
5. Coarsely chop the tuna and place it in sterilized jars. Now cover with oil, leaving a centimeter free from the edge of the jar.
6. With a knife, chop the tuna and make sure that it is completely soaked in oil. Add a bay leaf and three juniper berries to each jar.
7. Close the previously sterilized jars and put your tuna in oil in a cool and dry place. Wait at least a month before consuming it, for the tuna to flavor well with the oil and aromas.

Marmellata

CON BUCCIA DI LIMONE

SHOPPING LIST

- sugar (to taste)
- 20 lemons

DIRECTIONS

1. Remove the peel from the lemons, only the yellow part, and squeeze the juice.
2. Boil the peels in plenty of water, until they are tender. Drain and grind in a mortar, making a pulp.
3. Weigh the lemon juice previously obtained and add the sugar, respecting the following proportions: for 100 grams of juice, you must add 100 grams of sugar.
4. Boil sugar and lemon juice until the sugar is dissolved so that you will get a syrup. If necessary, add a few tablespoons of water.
5. At this point, add the flesh obtained from the skins of the lemons and cook for about an hour on a low heat, until the jam is ready.
6. Overrun when it's still hot and plug straight away.
7. Flip the pots over to create the vacuum, covering the jars with a blanket until they cool down.

Cozze
ALLA MARINARA

DIRECTIONS

1. Clean and brush the mussels, wash them carefully and leave them to soak after washing for half an hour in warm, salty water.
2. Spend half an hour putting them in a pot, without water and seasoning, and cook them over very low heat while continuing to stir. When the mussels have opened, drain them by collecting the cooking liquid in a bowl, and leave them aside.
3. Allow the mussels to cool and remove the shell once cold.
4. In a frying pan saute two cloves of garlic in plenty of olive oil, stir in the garlic, and add the water with vinegar and white wine and boil for five minutes over a very low heat.
5. Chop the parsley, basil, and red chilli and filter the cooking liquid of the mussels, set aside earlier.
6. Put it all in the pot and salt and pepper to your liking. Cook for another 70 minutes then turn off the heat and leave to cool.
7. Remove the garlic cloves and place them in the pots making sure that the mussels are completely covered by their cooking liquid. Tightly close the vessels and sterilize for an hour.

Moscardini
SOTT'ACETO

Tasty fish, fragrant as good as it preserves. It is excellently tasted preparation that will pay us well for our effort! Time 1 hour

DIRECTIONS

1. Clean and wash the moscardini very well, and cut them into pieces. If the moscardini are very small, you don't need to cut them.
2. Boil the white vinegar and water in equal parts, salt, and add the white wine and seasonings (laurel, onion, garlic, cloves, celery, and parsley).
3. Boil everything slowly, for a few minutes, then dip the moscardini. Cook for five minutes after which the heat is turned off and allow to cool in their cooking broth.
4. Drain and let it drain a little, then place in the oven already warm for a few minutes.
5. Leave to cool out of the oven and put in the pots with a few bay leaves and pepper. Cover with vinegar and store it in the cellar.

SHOPPING LIST

- 2 kg baby octopus
- some bay leaf
- 1 small bicna onion
- a few cloves garlic
- some clove carnation
- 1 piece white celery
- a few parsley tufts
- 1 glass white wine
- white vinegar
- olive oil
- Water
- sale

Alici Piccanti

Tasty, fragrant and very varied with fish preserves. These are a bit of a demanding preparation, but with excellent taste That will pay us a lot of for our effort! From classic mussels to marinara to tasty sea salad, to spicy anchovies: a series of proposals to satisfy every taste in fish!

🧺 SHOPPING LIST

- 1 kg anchovies in salt
- 3 glasses extra virgin olive oil
- 1 glass dry white wine
- 1 celery stalk
- 1 small carrot
- 1 cluded parsley
- 1 piece red chilli
- 1 jar pickled capers
- 1 sprig thyme
- 2 bay leaves

🍳 DIRECTIONS

1. Wash the anchovies in water and vinegar and spread them on a towel to dry for a few hours.
2. Chop all the aromas (celery, carrot, parsley, chilli, thyme, bay, and some caper) until reduced to mush.
3. Put everything in a pot, add the wine and oil and cook over very low heat for half an hour. If the sauce dries too much, add some more white wine.
4. Roll the anchovies with a caper inside each one.
5. Turn off the sauce and let it cool.
6. Arrange the anchovies regularly in the pots, covering each layer with the sauce. You can start consuming them after a few days.

60
MINUTES

Zucchine sotto aceto

DIRECTIONS

1. Wash the courgettes thoroughly, and dry them. Cut them in half and then cut them back into slices by the length

2. Pour the two glasses of vinegar into a pot, add a glass of water and salt. Cover and boil.

3. Remove the lid and dip the courgette pieces into the boiling liquid and blanch for two minutes. After the indicated time, collect the zucchini with a foam, drain them well and place them to dry on a towel (it will take about 3 hours), perfectly enlarged.

4. Peel the garlic cloves and slice them.

5. Clean the anchovies by scraping them with a knife and then rinsing them under water. Open them in half, remove the bone, and dry them.

6. Place the zucchini in the pots by interspersed with the anchovies and garlic cloves. Cover completely with oil and close the pots.

7. Sterilize and store in the pantry in the cool and dark for at least a month before consumption.

SHOPPING LIST

- 1 kg courgettes
- 8 cloves garlic
- 8 anchovies, salted
- 2 glasses white wine vinegar
- 1 teaspoon coarse salt
- extra virgin olive oil

Marmellata
DI MELE

1. Wash and peel the apples, cut them into slices, and then into small pieces.
2. Put them in a saucepan with water, cook over low heat, just soak the water, add the lemon juice, grated zest or pieces, and sugar. Cook until the ingredients mix well.
3. After cooking, pour the jam into a clean, sterilized, and dry jar. Close and flip.
4. Store in a cool, dark place. Consume after a week.

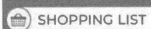

SHOPPING LIST

- 1 kg organic apples
- 1 organic lemon
- 400 - 500g whole brown sugar
- 1/2 cup water

Mele Secche

▣ DIRECTIONS

1. Prepare a bowl with plenty of water and the squeezed lemon.
2. Wash the apples, remove the core with the appropriate tool and cut them into slices half a cm thick horizontally.
3. Put the slices in the water and lemon so they will remain nice and clear.
4. Take some kitchen string and thread the apple slices, hang the string, and space the slices with laundry clothespins. Be careful because the first half hour drips a little on the ground, so put some newspaper sheets.
5. Leave them hanging for a few days, moving them from time to time and moving the laundry clothespins.
6. When they completely lose moisture and become dry, store them in a bread bag.

20

Marmellata
DI CAROTE

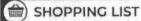

DIRECTIONS

1. Wash the carrots, tick them, and scrape them. Cut them into pieces, removing the soul.
2. Scrape the zest of 3 untreated lemons.
3. In a little unsalted water, cook the carrots. When they are soft and still hot, drain and sieve them or with a minipiner.
4. Add the sugar and skins of the grated lemons and put them back on the heat. Cook over a very gentle heat, stirring often.
5. When a drop of jam placed on the plate does not slip, remove it from the heat and let it cool down.
6. Then add the Rum and vanilla. Mix very well and overrun.
7. Allow it to cool completely before closing tightly and sterilize for 30 minutes from the time of the boil.
8. They must be completely covered with water and wrapped in a cloth to avoid breaking the jars containing your carrot jam.

Marmellata
DI CIPOLLE ROSSE

SHOPPING LIST

- 450g red onions
- 75 ml aceto balsamico
- 1 glass of wine aged or cognac
- 350g sugar

DIRECTIONS

1. Clean and slice as thinly as possible the onions, cover them with balsamic vinegar, cognac, and half the sugar and let them macerate for at least 2 hours.
2. Then place them in a saucepan and put them on the heat until they have wilted.
3. At this point, add the other half of the sugar, then boil. Always stir well, and cook until they are well-mixed.
4. To check the cooking point of the jam, make the traditional test of the saucer: put a teaspoon of compote on the plate and tilt it, if it does not slip away with ease, the jam is ready.
5. Place it still boiling in the jars already prepared and sterilized.
6. Close with the caps and flip the jars, cover them with a cloth and leave them until they have cooled completely.
7. At this point, wrap the cold jars with clean napkins and put them in a pot, cover them entirely with cold water and boil them for 20 minutes from the beginning of the first boil.
8. After 20 minutes, turn off the heat, let the water cool, then pull out the jars. Dry and store them in a cool, dark place.

Sgombri
IN VASO

1. Clean the mackerel and remove their heads and entrails
2. If you have a large pot, arrange the mackerel in it.
3. Cover with cold water, add salt and vinegar and place everything on the heat over high heat, and then boil.
4. When boiling, turn down the heat and boil slowly for three hours.
5. While the fish boils, prepare an axis of raw wood, covering it with a towel.
6. After three hours, remove the fish and peel them.
7. Put the fillets obtained from the previously prepared axis and cover everything with kitchen paper, and store them in a cool and dry place. They should dry for at least 24 hours.
8. Then arrange the fillets in the glass jars, taking care not to break them. Add seed oil until covered and a bay leaf for each pot.
9. Seal and place the pots to boil to reach the vacuum (usually it takes 5 minutes of boiling).
10. Remove the pots from the water when they have cooled. They could be eaten after at least three months of aging. They are also preserved for more than a year.
11. If you want to make mackerel naturally, once boiled, put them in warm pots, and cover them with cooking water. Then plug the jars and proceed to vacuum them.

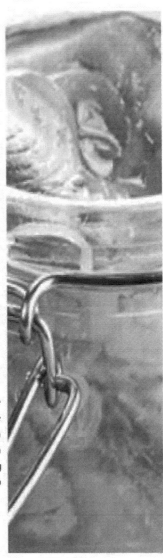

Gelatina di Maiale

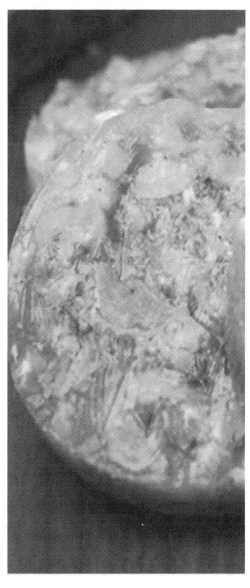

🧺 SHOPPING LIST

- 1/2 pork head
- 3 kg mixed pork (bacon, thigh and shoulder)
- 5 bay leaves
- 5 garlic cloves
- 1/2 litre vinegar
- ground red pepper (to taste)
- salt (to taste)

🗂 DIRECTIONS

1. Cut the pork head into large pieces and wash them. Cut the meat and wash it. Cover everything with cold water and boil.
2. When cooked, remove the meat and make sure to set aside the water.
3. When the meat is cold, cut into small pieces eliminating the bones.
4. After doing this, put the meat in a large pot with half cooking water and the remaining ingredients.
5. Cook for 1/2 hour, then put in the containers and store in the fridge.
6. After it has thickened, it is ready to eat.
7. PS: If you want to store long after cooking, put in jars and boil in a water bath for 45 minutes

24

Conserva

PER BRODO VEGETABLE

DIRECTIONS

1. Put all the ingredients and vegetables in the mixer and chop them finely.
2. Pour into a pan, add the oil and salt, and boil over very low heat for 20 - 30 minutes, stirring often.
3. Leave to cool, switch to the mixer again until you get a cream.
4. Store in the freezer in glass jars.

SHOPPING LIST

- 250g green sedane
- 2 medium carrots
- 2 medium onions
- 2-3 garlic cloves
- 2 bay leaves
- 1 sprig rosemary
- 2 sage tufts
- 1 bunch parsley
- 3 tbsp extra virgin olive oil
- 250g salt
- 300 gr extra virgin olive oil
- 1 double tomato concentrate tube

Melanzane
SOTT'OLIO

🧺 SHOPPING LIST

- round eggplant
- Herbs
- salt to taste
- Garlic
- leaves bay leaf
- olio d'oliva extra vergine

📖 DIRECTIONS

1. Wash the eggplant very well and peel at the thickness of 5 millimeters, taking care that all the slices keep the peel on the outside.
2. Sprinkle them abundantly with salt and leave them in a perforated container for an hour.
3. After this time, wash the slices under running water, take care not to tear them. Dry and brush them with herb oil and grill them at the right point on a steak or grill.
4. Gently chop them with chopped herbs, add salt, and press them in glass jars, remaining a few centimeters below the edge, with peppercorns and lauro leaves.
5. Cover them with oil and leave them overnight.
6. The next day, if necessary add oil, close the pots, and bring them safely to the pantry.

Chianti's tuna
(TONNO DEL CHIANTI)

SHOPPING LIST

- Pork (loin) 1 pound
- Dry white wine 1
- Laurel 6 leaves
- Juniper 3 berries
- Pepper in grains
- Rosemary 4 sprigs
- 1 sprig of rosemary
- Coarse salt to taste
- Extra virgin olive oil to taste
- Water 9 ounce

DIRECTIONS

Remove the fatty parts of the meat and cut it into pieces of about 5-6 centimeters.

Put the meat in a bowl and cover it with coarse salt, letting it rest for 3 days.

After the purging time, wash the meat under cold running water. Boil the wine with 9 ounces of water, and add 2 bay leaves, juniper berries, and pepper.

Put the meat in the pan and cook for 5 hours over low heat.

Turn off the heat and let it cool completely in the cooking liquid.

Drain the meat and fray it with your hands without making too small pieces. Fill the jars alternating the meat with some rosemary and bay leaves. Pour plenty of extra virgin olive oil, making sure that the meat is perfectly covered. Close the jars and refrigerate for up to one month.

Caramelize Figs
(FICHI CARAMELLATI)

Caramelized figs are a truly delicious homemade preserve that can be enjoyed both as an appetizer, in combination with salty ingredients such as bacon, salami, or gorgonzola, and a dessert version: with mascarpone cream, whipped ricotta, or ice cream.

DIRECTIONS

1. Gently clean 2 pounds of ripe but firm green figs with a damp absorbent paper. Using the potato peeler, cut into strips of untreated lemon and untreated orange.

2. Arrange the figs in a pan, making sure not to overlap them. Sprinkle them with 7 ounce of sugar and add the lemon and orange peel. Cover them with a cloth and let them macerate overnight so that they will release their liquid.

3. The next day, place the pan with the figs on fire and boil for about 1 minute; finish cooking in a preheated oven at 180 ° C for 10-15 minutes until the citrus-scented base liquid begins to caramelize

4. Let the figs cool, then distribute them in 4 jars, cleaned and dried, add a few pieces of cinnamon in each. Close the jars tightly and place them in a pot filled with cold water to cover them for at least 4-5 cm.

5. Proceed to sterilization by boiling the jars over medium heat for about 50-55 minutes. Turn off the heat and let it cool in the pot full of water. When the jars with the preserves are cold, dry them and decorate them as desired. Caramelized figs can be stored for up to 3 months.

Exotic Fruit Jam

MARMELLATA DI FRUTTA ESOTICA ALLA CITRONELLA

SHOPPING LIST

- 1.8 pounds of mango
- 14 ounce of papaya
- 10.6 ounce of pineapple
- 1.5 pounds of sugar
- 1 lemon
- 1 piece lemongrass (lemongrass)

🕐 **Preparation time : 1 hour 20 minutes**

DIRECTIONS

1. To prepare 3 x 14 ounce jars of lemongrass exotic fruit jam, first squeeze 1 lemon to obtain the juice. Cut 1 lemongrass stick into slices. Cut 1.8 pounds of mango pulp into cubes, 14 ounce of papaya pulp into slices, and 10.6 ounce of pineapple pulp into wedges.

2. Put all the exotic fruit in a saucepan, add the lemon juice and lemongrass, sprinkle with 1.5 pounds of sugar, mix and let it rest for 3 hours.

3. Cook the exotic fruit jam over low heat for an hour, stirring occasionally. Transfer the boiling jam into the sterilized jars, cover them, turn them upside down, let them cool, then turn them over again and keep them in a cool place.

Preparation time : 30 minutes

Stuffed Peppers

(PEPERONCINI ALLA PIEMONTESE)

The hot peppers stuffed Piemontese style are a specialty that can hardly be resisted. With a soft heart of tuna, anchovies, and capers in oil, they are a traditional preserve prepared in the summer when the peppers are ripe and easy to find. The recipe is very simple, and the ways to taste these peppers in oil are many: they are perfect for a homemade aperitif with friends, as a delicious appetizer or can be combined with cheeses such as robiola, stracchino, or goat cheese which, with their creaminess, reduce its spiciness. But why not also accompany them with grilled or boiled meats?

 **SHOPPING LIST**

- 60 hot pepper
- 8 green olives
- 320 gr tuna
- 3.5 ounce of anchovies or salted anchovies
- 2 tablespoons salted caper
- 1 quart of extra virgin olive oil
- 1 quart of apple vinegar
- 1 quart of white wine
- 1 tablespoon coarse salt, parsley to taste,

DIRECTIONS

1. For 5 jars of 3-4 dl of stuffed peppers Piedmont style, first wash 60 hot peppers and remove the stalk, the ribs, and the seeds. Boil 1 liter of white wine and 1 liter of vinegar with 1 tablespoon of coarse salt; add the peppers, cook for a minute, drain with a slotted spoon; put them upside down on a cloth and let them dry for 2 hours.

2. Desalt 3.5 ounce of salted anchovies under-water, fillet them, and remove the bones. Desalt 2 tablespoons of capers and chop coarsely. Blend the capers, 3.5 ounce of anchovies, 8 pitted green olives, and 11 ounce of drained tuna in oil in a blender. Add 1 tablespoon of very finely chopped parsley to the mixture.

3. Add the hot peppers to the mixture; place them in the previously washed jars and let them dry carefully; cover them with extra virgin olive oil and place the special plastic grids on top. Close and sterilize them in a pot with boiling water for 20 minutes. Let them cool in the water, then remove them and place them in a cool and dark place for about 3 months. When sealed, they keep for about 15 months. After opening, consume them within 15 days.

Stuffed peppers with tuna, anchovies and capers

(PERONCINI AL TONNO)

🕐 Preparation time : 35 minutes

🕐 Cooking TIME : 5 minutes

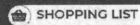

🧺 **SHOPPING LIST**

- 1 pound of chili pepper
- 9 ounce of canned tuna in oil
- 6 anchovies or anchovies
- 1 tablespoon salted caper
- 2 cloves of garlic, bay leaf to taste
- parsley to taste
- black pepper in grains to taste
- white wine to taste
- extra virgin olive oil to taste.

1. To prepare 3 pints jar of stuffed peppers, get 1 pound of hot round red peppers, remove the seeds, wash them, and blanch them for 3 minutes in the vinegar with a few bays leaves peppercorns and 1 clove of garlic crushed. Drain them and leave them on a towel upside down for 12 hours until dry.

2. Blend 9 ounce of tuna in oil with anchovies, desalted capers, and parsley. Add the hot peppers with the filling upwards, alternating them with slices of garlic and a little parsley.

3. Add extra virgin olive oil to the sterilized jar, wait 1 hour and pour more up to the level, seal tightly, and store it for at least 1 month. The right combination with chilies stuffed with tuna, anchovies, and capers is country bread and cheese.

Pear jam with chocolate

MARMELLATA PERE E CIOCCOLATO

Preparation time : 2 hours

Cooking TIME : 1 hour

SHOPPING LIST

· 7 pounds of pear
· 1 pound of sugar

· 7 tablespoons of bitter cocoa
· 1 small glass of rum

Pear jam with chocolate, an original and delicious compote to be enjoyed spread on a slice of brioche bread or as a filling for croissants, donuts, biscuits, and homemade tarts

DIRECTIONS

Prepare the fruit. Wash 7 pound of ripe pears, dry them well, peel them, divide them into quarters, core them, and cut them into slices. You should get 4 to 5 pounds of clean pears.

Put them in a saucepan with a thick bottom or with a non-stick coating, add 1 pound of sugar (including cane), mix with a wooden spoon, then let them macerate for 1 hour. Make a fruit puree.

Pass the macerated pears in a vegetable mill mounted with a disc with medium holes; collecting the puree in a bowl. Alternatively, you can also rely on an immersion blender. Add the cocoa. When whisking, add 6-7 tablespoons of unsweetened cocoa powder dropped from a sieve to the purée of pears to avoid the formation of lumps. When you have obtained a homogeneous mixture, transfer it to the saucepan in which you have macerated the pears. Cook and fill the jars.

Put the mixture on the stove and cook over low heat for 1 hour, stirring often. Add 1 glass of rum and leave on the fire until the jam has thickened. Then divide the boiling jam into well-washed jars, sterilized in boiling water, and then dried, close them with the lid, turn them upside down and let them cool overnight.

Preserve. When the jars with the chocolate pear jam are completely cold, put them in the pantry. If you like, you can add 50 g of chopped almonds to the jam. In this case, cooking will be a little faster because almonds are a good thickener.

Watermelon jam

(CONFETTURA DI ANGURIA)

SHOPPING LIST

- 3 pounds of watermelon
- 2 pounds of sugar
- 1 small glass of brandy
- 1 vanilla or vanillin sachet

DIRECTIONS

1) To prepare a delicious homemade watermelon jam, first, marinate 3 pounds of chopped and seedless watermelon pulp for 12 hours with 2 pounds of sugar and a glass of brandy.

2) Drain the fruit and boil the juice until you get syrup. Add the watermelon and 1 sachet of vanilla and cook until the right consistency.

3) Pour your still hot watermelon jam into previously sterilized glass jars, close with the appropriate cap, and let it cool with the containers turned upside down. Store in a dark, cool, and dry place.

Zucchini jam

(MARMELLATA DI ZUCCHINE)

SHOPPING LIST

- 2 pounds of courgette
- 1.8 pounds of sugar
- 5 dl natural mineral water
- 1 vanilla stick
- 1 lemon juice
- 4 tablespoons

DIRECTIONS

Zucchini jam is a summer jam based on vegetables rather than fruit. Although it is delicious, it is prepared in relatively few minutes and is perfect to accompany cheese platters, fresh or seasoned, and mixed cold cuts or main courses based on both fish and meat.

1) Wash 2 pounds of courgettes, peel and cut them into very thin strips. Boil 1 pint of water with 1.8 pounds of sugar. Cook the liquid over very low heat, constantly stirring, until you get a thick and homogeneous syrup.

2) Add the courgettes, the juice of 1 lemon, and 1 vanilla pod or 1 teaspoon of vanilla powder and continue cooking over medium heat, constantly stirring, for 30 minutes.

3) Add 4 tablespoons of Cognac into the zucchini jam, then pour it still hot into well-cleaned glass jars heated in a bain-marie. Seal the jars hermetically, sterilize them by boiling them, then place the jam in a cool and dry place for 1 month.

Mushrooms alla pizzaiola with capers and anchovies

(FUNGHI ALLA PIZZAIOLA)

🧺 SHOPPING LIST

- 1 pound of porcini mushrooms
- to taste white vinegar
- to taste basil
- 2 anchovies or anchovies
- to taste extra virgin olive oil
- 1.8 ounce of dried tomatoes cognac
- 1 tablespoon salted caper

💼 DIRECTIONS

1) Clean 1 pound of very fresh porcini mushrooms very carefully and cut them into small pieces.

2) Boil 2 quarts of water in a pot with half glass of vinegar. Add the mushrooms and blanch them for 15 seconds, then drain them well and let them dry on a clean cloth for at least half an hour.

3) Transfer the mushrooms to a bowl and add 1.8 ounce of dried tomatoes, 2 anchovy fillets in oil, 1 sprig of basil, and 1 tablespoon of salted capers. Mix well and place the mushrooms in sterilized glass jars.

4) Now, pour the oil and mash them with a fork to be well covered with oil and let out the air bubbles.

5) Close them tightly and put them in a cool and dry place for at least a week before enjoying them.

Flavored oil
(OLIO AROMATIZZATO)

SHOPPING LIST

- 1 pint of extra virgin olive oil to taste the chili
- to taste garlic
- to taste herbs.

DIRECTIONS

1) For the quick heat recipe, wash 1 bunch of basil, dry it, and put it in a heat-resistant bottle. Add 1 clove of unpeeled garlic, 1 piece of hot pepper, 1 lemon zest, and 6 black peppercorns. Pour 1 pint extra virgin olive oil and close. Fill a saucepan 1/3 full with water and heat until hot but not boiling. Put the bottle in place and leave it until the water cools. Remove it from the casserole, let it rest for 5 days, and filter.

2) For the cold recipe with a long waiting time, put 1 pint of extra virgin olive oil in a bottle or a jar with a couple of bay leaves, sage, 1 sprig of tarragon, 1 sprig of rosemary, and a couple of sprigs of thyme. Add a few cloves of whole garlic and, if you like spicy flavors, even a couple of whole chilies. Seal tightly and let it rest for a month before use.

3) For a flavored oil used to grease the fish and vegetable skewers before grilling, add 1 sprig of rosemary, 2-3 peppercorns, 3 cloves of garlic, and coarse salt. For a flavored oil more suitable for mixed meat skewers: leave 3 peeled garlic cloves, 1 chili pepper, a few juniper berries, and little peppercorns to macerate in the usual quantity of oil. Filter after 7 days.

Walnut sauce

(SALSA DI NOCI CON ROSMARINO E PARMIGIANO)

(🕐) **Preparation time : 30 minutes**

(🛒) **SHOPPING LIST**

- 9 ounce of walnut kernels
- 1.5 dl extra virgin
- 3 ounce of parmesan
- to taste Salt to taste
- pepper
- 5 cloves of garlic
- 1 sprig of rosemary

1) For 1 jar of 4 dl of walnut sauce, first dip a few walnut kernels at a time in boiling water, then drain with a perforated scoop and peel them. For the sauce to have a more delicate taste, peel at least half of the kernels.

2) Dry the kernels well on a cloth or place them briefly in the oven at no more than 100 °C in ventilated mode, leaving the door slightly open.

3) Transfer the walnut kernels to the mixer together with 3 ounce of grated Parmesan cheese, 1/2 clove of peeled garlic, and a handful of rosemary needles. Add a pinch of salt and pepper, then operate the appliance, pouring half the oil a little at a time. Continue to blend and add the remaining oil until the sauce is not too smooth or fluid inconsistency

4) Transfer the walnut sauce with rosemary and parmesan in an airtight glass jar, previously cleaned and dried, and store it in a cool and dark place: it can be kept for 8-10 days at the most.

Homemade dried figs

(FICHI SECCHI FATTI IN CASA)

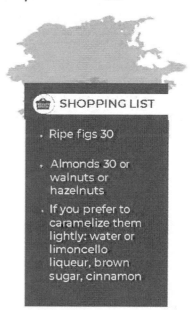

🧺 SHOPPING LIST

- Ripe figs 30

- Almonds 30 or walnuts or hazelnuts

- If you prefer to caramelize them lightly: water or limoncello liqueur, brown sugar, cinnamon

🍳 DIRECTIONS

Gently wash the figs and dry them with a clean cloth. Cut them in half without detaching them (to create the pair) lengthwise. Arrange them on a tray lined with parchment paper or on a trellis (see photo) and expose them to the sun and turn them 2/3 times a day. Cover the tray with a net to keep insects away. Put the figs inside at sunset to avoid the humidity of the night, which would lengthen drying times. The following day, expose them to the sun again. The figs will be ready after about 2/3 days, and they will have lost moisture and will be darker and withered. At this point, stuff each pair of figs with walnut kernels or toasted hazelnuts, pieces of lemon, or cedar peel if desired. Close the pair and place them on a baking sheet lined with parchment paper. Place the baking sheet in a preheated oven at 180°C for about 10/15 minutes, just long enough to brown them. To make them more delicious, you can caramelize them lightly: after filling the figs with hazel-nuts or walnuts, close them and place them on the baking sheet lined with parchment paper. In a bowl, add a few tablespoons of water or limoncello liqueur, dissolve a tablespoon of brown or granulated sugar and a pinch of cinnamon, mix well, brush the surface of the figs thoroughly and bake for about 20 minutes (they must brown). Keep the figs well-dried in a glass jar or vacuum bags.

CHAPTER2
WATER BATH RECIPES

Water Bath Recipes: Fruits and Vegetables

Apple Chutney

Preparation Time: 10 minutes
Cooking Time: 90 minutes
Servings: 8 11-ounce jars
Ingredients:

- 2 cups white vinegar
- 2 teaspoons salt
- 2 tablespoons ground cinnamon
- 2 tablespoons ground ginger
- 2 cups white sugar
- 2 cups brown sugar
- 1 lb. raisins
- 2 jalapeno peppers, chopped
- 1 cup onions, chopped
- 10 medium apples, cored and chopped

Directions:

Combine ingredients into a thick-bottomed pot and simmer until thick for about 1 hour.

Ladle into sterilized jars, leaving about 1/2-inch at the top of jars. Process jars by submerging in a water bath for 20 minutes.

Remove the jars then place on a tea towel to cool.

Nutrition: 43 kCal

Canned Blueberries

Preparation Time:20 minutes
Cooking Time:90 minutes
Servings:6 11-ounce jars
Ingredients:

    8 cups blueberries
    2 cups sugar

Directions:
Place the blueberries into a thick-bottomed pot and cover them with sugar. Let stand for 1 hour.
Set to medium heat and cook for 10 minutes, until blueberries release juices. Once that
happens, turn off the heat and ladle berries into hot sterilized jam jars.
Wipe the rims and secure them on jars. Totally submerge into a boiling water bath for 20
minutes. Remove jars and place them on top of a tea towel to cool.
Nutrition:215 kCal

Canned Cherries

Preparation Time:10 minutes
Cooking Time: 60 minutes
Servings:8 11-ounce jar
Ingredients:

    1-quart water
    3 cups sugar
    5lbs. cherries pitted

Directions:
Using a saucepan, dissolve the sugar in hot water.
After this, add cherries into the pan and mix. Ladle into sterilized jars, leaving 1/2-inch space at
the top of jars.
Clean rims and secure on jars.
Totally submerge jars in a boiling water bath for 45 minutes. Remove the jars then place on a
tea towel to cool.
If you want to can cherry pie filling, heat the cherries and simmer for 10 minutes before placing
them into jam jars.
Nutrition:149 kCal

Red Grapes

Preparation Time: 20 minutes
Cooking Time: 0 minutes
Servings: 1-quart jar
Ingredients:

- 1 lb. Red grapes
- ¼ teaspoon cloves
- ½ vanilla bean
- 1 cinnamon stick
- 1 cup sugar
- ¼ cup water
- 1 cup apple cider vinegar
- ¼ teaspoon black peppercorns
- 1/8 teaspoon yellow mustard seed

Directions:

Begin by washing the grapes and removing the stem.

Remove the end that was attached to the stem, then set aside.

Place the vinegar, water, and sugar into a saucepan over high heat and boil.

Place all of the spices in the bottom of a 1-quart jar. Place the grapes in the jar. Pour the brine over the grapes and place the lid onto the jar.

Allow the used jar to cool, then place in the fridge to rest for 24 hours.

Nutrition: 152 kCal

Password: pub620

Prunes

Preparation Time: 15 minutes
Cooking Time: 20 minutes
Servings: 1-quart jar
Ingredients:

- 1 bay leaf
- 1-star anise
- 3 allspice berries
- 4 green cardamom pods
- 1/8 teaspoon red chili flakes
- ¼ teaspoon cloves
- ¼ teaspoon black peppercorns
- 1 teaspoon ginger, grated
- ¼ cup honey
- ¼ cup brown sugar
- 1 blood orange, with the zest, removed
- 1 cup red wine vinegar
- 1 lb. Prunes pitted
- Pinch of salt

Directions:

Begin by mixing the prunes and red wine vinegar in a medium saucepan.

Add in the blood orange zest also the juice from the blood orange, and mix ingredients.

Simmer for 20 minutes. Remove from heat.

Allow the prunes to cool, then add them into the jar.

Clean the lid and secure it on the jar. Place the jar in the fridge once it is has cooled at room temperature.

Nutrition: 246 kCal

Cranberries

Preparation Time: 30 minutes
Cooking Time: 20-30 minutes
Servings: 4 11-ounce jars
Ingredients:

- 24-ounces cranberries
- 1 teaspoon allspice
- 2 cinnamon sticks
- 3 cups sugar
- 3 cups apple cider vinegar
- ¼ teaspoon juniper berries
- ½ teaspoon black peppercorns
- ½ teaspoon cloves

Directions:

Begin by washing cranberries and removing any bad cranberries or stems.

Mix the sugar and vinegar and bring to a boil in a saucepan over medium heat. Add in the cinnamon sticks.

Place the allspice, juniper berries, peppercorns, and cloves in a spice bag. Place the bag in the brine. Once the brine begins to boil, add in the cranberries and stir.

Allow to cook for 7 minutes.

After cooking, remove the mix from heat and take out the spice bag and cinnamon sticks.

Break both cinnamon sticks in half, and set them aside.

Using a spoon, remove the cranberries from the brine and place them into jars. Pour the brine over the cranberries.

Leave about 1/2-inch of space at the top of jars. Place ½ a cinnamon stick into each jar. Clean the lids then secure them on jars.

Totally submerge jars in a boiling water bath for 10 minutes.

After this, remove the jars and place them on a tea towel to cool. Once they are not too hot, store them in the fridge. Let them sit for 24 hours.

Nutrition: 158 kCal

Watermelon Pickles

Preparation Time: 30 minutes
Cooking Time: 1 hour and 20 minutes
Servings: 4-5 11-ounce jars
Ingredients:

- 2 teaspoons cloves
- 15-inches cinnamon sticks, broken into pieces
- 1 ½ cups water
- 1 ½ cups white vinegar
- 6 cups water
- 1 10 pound watermelon
- 1/3 cup pickling salt
- 3 ½ cup sugar

Directions:

Remove the rind from the watermelon, then trim the pale outer portions. Discard.

Cut the watermelon into 1-inch chunks; you should have about 9 cups. Place the watermelon chunks into a large non-metal mixing bowl.

Mix 6 cups of water and pickling salt. Pour over the watermelon and soak it overnight. Pour the watermelon into a colander and rinse with cold water. Place the watermelon in a 4-quart pot and cover it with cold water.

Boil the mixture. Reduce heat and simmer for 25 minutes.

Place 1 ½ cups water, vinegar, cinnamon sticks, sugar, and cloves in a pot and boil. Reduce heat and cook for 10 minutes. Strain and reserve the liquid.

Add the watermelon to the syrup and boil. Reduce the heat to a simmer for 30 minutes and cover.

Place the watermelon and the syrup in jars, leaving 1/2-inch of space at the top of the jars.

Totally submerge the jars in a water bath for 10 minutes.

Remove jars and place on a tea towel to cool.

Nutrition: 70 kCal

Blueberry Pie Filling

Preparation Time: 15 minutes
Cooking Time: 45 minutes
Servings: 6 11-ounce jars
Ingredients:

> 6 cups fresh blueberries
> ½ cup lemon juice
> 7 cups cold water
> 6 cups sugar

Directions:

Wash and drain blueberries.

In a large pot, bring blueberries and enough water, cover them and boil for 5 minutes. After this, drain. Using a large pot, combine the sugar, lemon juice, water, and fruit pectin and boil. Stir in the blueberries, then remove from the heat.

Pour the mixture into sterilized jars, leaving a ½ inch on top of the jars.

Clean the rims then secure them to jars. Totally submerge the jars in a boiling water bath for 25 minutes. Remove the jars and place them on the counter to cool.

Nutrition: 474kCal

Apple Pie Filling

Preparation Time: 15 minutes
Cooking Time: 45 minutes
Servings: 4 11-ounce jars
Ingredients:

> 5 cups lemon juice
> ¾ cup nutmeg (optional)
> 2 ½ cups apple juice
> 1 tablespoon cold water
> 1 ½ cups cinnamon
> 5 ½ cups fruit pectin
> 6 cups sugar
> 7 fresh apples, blanched and sliced

Directions:

In a large pot, cook the apples in 6 cups of boiling water for 5 minutes then drain.

In another pot, combine fruit pectin, sugar, and cinnamon with the water and apple juice. Bring it to a boil after which, add the nutmeg.

When the mixture begins to thicken, add the lemon juice and cook for 1 minute. Ladle into sterilized jars, leaving about 1/2-inch at the top of jars.

Clean rims and lids then secure onto jars. Allow jars to cool on the counter.

Nutrition: 74 kCal

Cinnamon Banana Butter

Preparation Time: 15 minutes
Cooking Time: 30 minutes
Servings: 2 11-ounce jars
Ingredients:

- ½ teaspoon ground cinnamon
- 3 teaspoons vanilla
- 4 ½ cups sugar
- 1 package fruit pectin
- 1/3 cup fresh lemon juice
- 4 cups mashed bananas

Directions:

In a saucepan, mix lemon juice, bananas, and pectin until the pectin is dissolved. Bring to a boil, stirring constantly. Stir in the sugar.

Stirring constantly heat to a full rolling boil; then remove the pan from heat and mix in vanilla and cinnamon.

Ladle into sterilized jars, leaving about 1/2-inch at the top of jars. Clean the rims and lids and secure them on jars. Totally submerge jars into boiling water bath for 10 minutes.

Remove the used jars and set them on a tea towel on the counter to cool.

Nutrition: 73kCal

Spicy Carrots

Preparation Time: 20 minutes
Cooking Time: 1 hour
Servings: 4-5 11-ounce jars
Ingredients:

- 2 pints fresh carrots
- 1 cup sugar
- 2 cups cider vinegar
- 1 ½ teaspoon celery seed
- ¼ piece mace
- ¼ stick cinnamon
- ¾ teaspoons cloves
- ¾ teaspoons allspice
- ¼ teaspoon salt

Directions:

Tie the salt and the spices in a thin cloth bag. Boil the sugar, vinegar, and spices for 15 minutes. Sterilize a quart jar for about fifteen minutes in boiling water. Remove sterilized jar from water then adds the vinegar mixture into it.

Clean the rim and lid and secure to jar and set aside for about 2 weeks.

Remove the spice bag. Cook the fresh carrots until they are tender but firm, and let them cool. Heat the vinegar add ½ cup of the carrot liquid. Add the carrots and simmer for 15 minutes. Pack sterilized jars with carrots and cover them with vinegar mixture. Stir to remove air bubbles. Clean rims and lids and secure to jars. Totally submerge jars in a boiling water bath for 10 minutes.

Nutrition: 15 kCal

Spicy Green Beans

Preparation Time: 20 minutes
Cooking Time: 1 hour
Servings: 2-3 11-ounce jars
Ingredients:

  2 pints green beans
  1 cup sugar
  2 cups cider vinegar
  1 ½ teaspoons celery seed
  ¼ piece mace
  ¼ stick cinnamon
  ¾ teaspoon allspice
  ¼ teaspoon salt

Directions:

Tie the salt and the spices in a thin cloth bag. Boil the sugar, vinegar, and spices for 15 minutes. Add mixture to a sterilized quart jar and secure lid and set aside for 2 weeks. Remove the spice bag. Cook fresh beans until firm but tender, and let them cool.

Heat the vinegar and add ½ cup of bean liquid. Add the beans. Simmer for 10 minutes.

Pack the beans into sterilized jars, and cover beans with vinegar mixture.

Remove air bubbles using a spoon and stir. Clean rims and lids then secure them onto jars. Totally submerge jars into boiling water bath for 10 minutes.

Remove the jars and place them onto a tea towel on the counter to cool.

Nutrition: 94 kCal

Spiced Beets

Preparation Time: 20 minutes
Cooking Time: 1 hour
Servings: 2-3 11-ounce jars
Ingredients:

   2 pints beets
   1 cup sugar
   2 cups cider vinegar
   1 ½ teaspoons celery seed
   ¼ piece mace
   ¼ stick cinnamon
   ¾ teaspoon cloves
   ¾ teaspoon allspice
   ¼ teaspoon salt

Directions:

Tie the salt and spices into a thin cloth bag. Boil the vinegar, spices, and sugar for 15 minutes. Pour mixture into a sterilized quart jar. Clean rim and lid and secure on to jar, then set aside for 2 weeks.

Remove the spice bag. Cook the beets until reaching tenderness but firm, then allow them to cool. Peel the beets. Heat the vinegar and add ½ cup beet liquid. Add the beets and simmer for 15 minutes.

Pack into sterilized jars, covering the beets with vinegar. Remove the air bubbles using a spoon, secure the lids. Totally submerge the jars into a boiling water bath for 10 minutes. After this, remove the jars and place them on a tea towel on the counter to cool.

Nutrition: 160 kCal

Marinated Fava Beans

Preparation Time: 20 minutes
Cooking Time: 1 hour
Servings: 4-5 11-ounce jars
Ingredients:

  ¼ teaspoon black ground pepper
  1 ½ lb. Fava beans
  2 tablespoons red wine vinegar
  ½ teaspoon kosher salt
  2 tablespoons olive oil
  1 teaspoon garlic, minced
  2 sprigs of fresh rosemary

Directions:

Allow the pot of salted water to a boil.

While the water is heating up, remove the beans from their pods.

Once the water is boiling add beans, and cook for about 3 minutes or until tender and green. Drain the beans. After which, rinse them under cold water.

Pop the Fava beans out of their casings, and set them aside.

Mix the olive oil in a mason jar with vinegar, garlic, rosemary sprigs, salt, and pepper.

Put the lid onto the jar then shake to combine contents. Add the Fava beans to the jar and secure the lid.

These marinated beans will keep up to 3 days in the fridge. Allow the beans to soak for at least 15 minutes in the mix before serving them.

Nutrition: 250 kCal

CHAPTER 3:

Water Bath Recipes: Preserves, Conserves, and Some Marmalades

Kumquats Marmalade
Preparation Time: 5 minutes
Cooking Time: 30 minutes
Servings: 2 (½ pint) jars
Ingredients:
　　½ cup sugar
　　2 cups kumquats, chopped
　　½ cup water
　　Pinch of ground cinnamon and ground cardamom
Directions:
Place kumquats into a pot. Add ground cinnamon, ground cardamom, sugar, and water then mix together. Cover it and let sit for 2 to 3 hours to allow the fruit to macerate or refrigerate overnight for more flavor.
Cook with medium-high heat using a pot heat and then bring mixture to a simmer, stirring continuously. Reduce heat to medium; cook and stir continuously for 10 minutes.

Remove from heat. Allow to cool, 5 to 10 minutes

Spoon warm marmalade into sterilized jars. Cover and let cool to room temperature. Refrigerate to chill.

Nutrition: 34.9 kCal

Super Tangy Marmalade

Preparation Time: 5 minutes

Cooking Time: 35 minutes

Servings: 3-4 (½ pint) jars

Ingredients:

>   3 ½ cups white granulated sugar
>   1 cup limes, unpeeled, and thinly sliced
>   1 cup lemons, unpeeled and thinly sliced
>   3 cups water

Direction:

In a deep saucepan or a cooking pot, combine the citrus slices and water.

Boil the mixture; simmer for a few minutes over low heat.

Mix in the sugar.

Boil the mixture till the thermometer reads 220°F; cook for about 25-30 minutes over medium heat until firm and thick. Stir continuously

Once done, pour the hot mixture into pre-sterilized jars using a jar funnel. Maintain a headspace of ¼ inch from the jar top.

To remove tiny air bubbles, use a nonmetallic spatula and stir it gently.

After this, wipe the sealing edges with a damp cloth. Then, close the jars with the lid. Also, adjust the bands/rings to seal and prevent any leakage.

Place the jars in a dry and dark place. Allow to cool.

Store in refrigerator and use within 10 days.

Nutrition: 41 kCal

Onion Garlic Marmalade

Preparation Time: 5 minutes
Cooking Time: 40 minutes
Servings: 2-3 (1 pint) jars
Ingredients:

- 4-5 cups sweet onions, thinly sliced
- 1 tablespoon red wine vinegar
- 1 ½ tablespoons brown sugar
- ½ tablespoon butter
- ½ teaspoon salt
- 2 garlic cloves, minced
- 1/8 teaspoon black pepper

Directions:

In a deep saucepan or a cooking pot, combine the sugar, onion, and garlic.

Boil the mixture; cook for about 25-30 minutes over medium heat. Stir continually. Mix in the vinegar, butter, salt, and pepper.

Boil the mixture until the thermometer reads 220°F; cook for 10-12 minutes over medium heat until firm and thick. Stir continuously.

After which, pour the hot mixture into pre-sterilized jars using a jar funnel. Maintain head-space of ¼ inch from the jar top. To remove tiny air bubbles, use a nonmetallic spatula and stir gently.

After this, wipe the edges with a damp cloth. Close the jars and adjust the bands/rings to seal and prevent any leakage.

Place the jars in a dry and dark place. Allow to cool.

Store the marmalade in a refrigerator and use it within 10 days.

Nutrition: 121 kCal

Ginger Orange Marmalade

Preparation Time: 20 minutes
Cooking Time: 1 hour and 20 minutes
Servings: 2-3 (1/2 pint) jars
Ingredients:

- 6-7 bitter oranges
- 2 cups of water
- 1 medium lemon
- 3 cups granulated sugar
- 1 ¼ tablespoons ginger, peeled, and grated

Directions:

Remove the oranges' and lemons' skins and cut them into strips.

Cut the oranges and lemons into halves. Juice, remove the seeds, and set aside the juice but do not discard the pulp.

In a deep saucepan or a cooking pot, combine the water, pulp, juice, and peels.

Boil the mixture; simmer for 45-50 minutes until the strips are softened

Mix in the sugar and ginger.

Boil the mixture till the thermometer reads 220°F; cook over medium heat until firm and thick. Stir continuously

Once done, pour the hot mixture into pre-sterilized jars using a jar funnel. Maintain a headspace of ¼ inch from the jar top.

To remove tiny air bubbles, use a nonmetallic spatula and stir it gently.

After this, wipe the sealing edges with a damp cloth. Then, close the jars. Also, adjust the bands/rings to seal and prevent any leakage.

Place the jars in a dry and dark place. Allow to cool.

Store in your refrigerator and use it within 10 days.

Nutrition: 73 kCal

Tangy Tomato Preserve

Preparation Time: 15 minutes
Cooking Time: 30 minutes
Servings: 3-4 (½ pint) jars
Ingredients:

- 1 cup sugar
- ¾ cup honey
- 2 medium lemons, unpeeled, chopped and seeded
- 2 ½ pounds yellow tomatoes
- 2 ounces ginger, grated

Directions:

In a deep saucepan or a cooking pot, combine the water and tomatoes.

Boil the mixture; simmer over low heat to soften tomatoes.

Remove the seeds and chop the tomatoes.

In a deep saucepan or a cooking pot, combine the chopped tomatoes, honey, and sugar.

Set aside for a few hours or you may choose to do it overnight.

Add the lemons and ginger.

Boil the mixture till the thermometer reads 220°F; cook over medium heat until firm and thick. Stir continuously

Once done, pour the hot mixture into pre-sterilized jars using a jar funnel. Maintain a headspace of ¼ inch from the jar top.

To remove tiny air bubbles, use a nonmetallic spatula and stir it gently.

After this, wipe the sealing edges with a damp cloth. Then, close the jars. Also, adjust the bands/rings to seal and prevent any leakage.

Place the jars in a dry and dark place. Allow to cool.

Store in your refrigerator and use it within 10 days.

Nutrition: 124 kCal

Black Currant Preserve

Preparation Time: 10 minutes
Cooking Time: 35 minutes
Servings: 4 (½ pint) jars
Ingredients:

  4 ½ cups black currants, crushed
  ¼ cup lemon juice
  3 cups granulated sugar
  1 cup water
  1 tablespoon lemon zest
  Pinch of salt

Directions:

In a deep saucepan or a cooking pot, combine the ingredients.

Boil the mixture till the thermometer reads 220°F; cook for about 30 minutes over medium heat until firm and thick. Stir continuously. Once done, pour the hot mixture into pre-sterilized jars using a jar funnel. Maintain a headspace of ¼ inch from the jar top.

To remove tiny air bubbles, use a nonmetallic spatula and stir it gently.

After this, wipe the sealing edges with a damp cloth. Then, close the jars. Also, adjust the bands/rings to seal and prevent any leakage. Place the jars in a dry and dark place. Allow to cool. Store in your refrigerator and use it within 10 days.

Nutrition: 52 kCal

Watermelon Lemon Preserves

Preparation Time: 15 minutes
Cooking Time: 2 hours and 30 minutes
Servings: 4 (½ pint) jars
Ingredients:

  2 pounds watermelon, peeled, seeded and cubed
  3 cups white sugar
  3 lemons unpeeled, sliced and seeded

Direction:

In a deep saucepan or a cooking pot, combine the watermelon cubes, lemons and sugar.

Boil the mixture; cook for about 2 hours over medium heat until fir and thick. Stir continuously.

Once done, pour the hot mixture into pre-sterilized jars using a jar funnel. Maintain a headspace of ¼ inch from the jar top. To remove tiny air bubbles, use a nonmetallic spatula and stir it gently. After this, wipe the sealing edges with a damp cloth. Then, close the jars. Also, adjust the bands/rings to seal and prevent any leakage.

Place the jars in a dry and dark place. Allow to cool.

Store in your refrigerator.

Nutrition: 224 kCal

Apple Lemon Preserve

Preparation Time: 5 minutes
Cooking Time: 15 minutes
Servings: 3-4 (½ pint) jars
Ingredients:

> 3 cups apples, peeled, cored and sliced
> ½ cup water
> ` teaspoon ground nutmeg
> ½ tablespoon lemon juice
> 1 lemon, unpeeled, seeded, and sliced
> 1 (1/75 ounce) package powdered pectin
> 2 cups sugar

Directions:

In a deep saucepan or a cooking pot, combine the water, sugar, lemon juice, lemon slices, and apples.

Boil the mixture; cook for about 8-10 minutes over medium heat until firm and thick. Stir continuously.

Mix in the pectin and nutmeg.

Boil the mixture until the thermometer reads 220°F; cook over medium heat until firm and thick. Stir continuously.

Once done, pour the hot mixture into pre-sterilized jars using a jar funnel. Maintain a head-space of ¼ inch from the jar top.

To remove tiny air bubbles, use a nonmetallic spatula and stir it gently.

After this, wipe the sealing edges with a damp cloth. Then, close the jars. Also, adjust the bands/rings to seal and prevent any leakage.

Put the used jars in a water bath for about 10 minutes

Place the jars in a dry and dark place. Allow to cool.

Store in your refrigerator

Nutrition: 50 kCal

Lemon Peach Preserve
Preparation Time: 15 minutes
Cooking Time: 1 hour and 30 minutes
Servings: 4 (½ pint) jars
Ingredients:
    Juice of 2 large lemons
    3 pounds peaches, peeled, pitted, and cubed
    1 ½ cups granulated sugar
Directions:
In a deep saucepan or a cooking pot, combine the peaches, lemon juice and sugar.
Set the mixture aside for 2-4 hours.
Boil the mixture till the thermometer reads 220°F; cook for about 1-2 hours over medium heat until firm and thick. Stir continuously
Once done, pour the hot mixture into pre-sterilized jars using a jar funnel. Maintain a headspace of ¼ inch from the jar top.
To remove tiny air bubbles, use a nonmetallic spatula and stir it gently.
After this, wipe the sealing edges with a damp cloth. Then, close the jars. Also, adjust the bands/rings to seal and prevent any leakage.
Put the used jars in a water bath for about 10 minutes
Place the jars in a dry and dark place. Allow to cool.
Store in your refrigerator.
Nutrition: 50 kCal

Pear Ginger Preserve

Preparation Time: 10 minutes
Cooking Time: 20 minutes
Servings: 3-4 (1/2 pint) jars
Ingredients:

- 4 cups pears. Peeled, seeded, and chopped
- ½ teaspoon salt
- 2 ½ cups honey
- 1 lemon, peeled and diced

Direction:

In a deep saucepan or a cooking pot, combine the ingredients.

Boil the mixture till the thermometer reads 220°F; cook for about 12-15 minutes over medium heat until firm and thick. Stir continuously

Once done, pour the hot mixture into pre-sterilized jars using a jar funnel. Maintain a headspace of ¼ inch from the jar top.

To remove tiny air bubbles, use a nonmetallic spatula and stir it gently.

After this, wipe the sealing edges with a damp cloth. Then, close the jars. Also, adjust the bands/rings to seal and prevent any leakage.

Place the jars in a dry and dark place. Allow to cool.

Store in your refrigerator and use it within 10 days.

Nutrition: 50 kCal

Cantaloupe Peach Conserve

Preparation Time: 5 minutes
Cooking Time: 40 minutes
Servings: 3-4 (½ pint) jars
Ingredients:

¼ cup blanched almonds, coarsely chopped
1 ½ cups cantaloupe, chopped
1 ½ cups peaches, peeled and chopped
2 cups sugar
½ tablespoon lemon juice
¼ teaspoon ground nutmeg
1/8 teaspoon salt
1/8 teaspoon grated orange rind

Directions:

In a deep saucepan or a cooking pot, combine the cantaloupe and peaches.

Boil the mixture; cook for about 10 minutes. Stir continuously.

Stir in sugar and lemon juice.

Boil the mixture and then stir in the remaining ingredients.

Boil the mixture till the thermometer reads 220°F; cook for about 10-12 minutes over medium heat until firm and thick. Stir continuously

Once done, pour the hot mixture into pre-sterilized jars using a jar funnel. Maintain a headspace of ¼ inch from the jar top.

To remove tiny air bubbles, use a nonmetallic spatula and stir it gently.

After this, wipe the sealing edges with a damp cloth. Then, close the jars. Also, adjust the bands/rings to seal and prevent any leakage.

Put in a water bath for around 10-15 minutes.

Place the jars in a dry and dark place. Allow to cool.

Store in your refrigerator.

Nutrition: 117 kCal

Cranberry Apple Conserve

Preparation Time: 15 minutes
Cooking Time: 20 minutes
Servings: 3-4 (1/2 pint) jars
Ingredients:

- 1 Granny Smith apple, peeled, cored, and also cut into small pieces
- Zest and juice of 1 orange
- Zest and juice of 1 lemon
- 1 ½ cups fresh cranberries
- 1 ¾ cups sugar
- ¾ cup chopped walnuts or pecans
- ¾ cup raisins
- 1 cup water

Directions:

In a deep saucepan or a cooking pot, combine the water, cranberries, and sugar.

Boil the mixture and simmer for 5 minutes, stirring continuously.

Mix in the juice, zest, and apple.

Boil the mixture till the thermometer reads 220°F; cook for about 15 minutes over medium heat until firm and thick. Stir continuously

Mix in the nuts and raisins.

Once done, pour the hot mixture into pre-sterilized jars using a jar funnel. Maintain a headspace of ¼ inch from the jar top.

To remove tiny air bubbles, use a nonmetallic spatula and stir it gently.

After this, wipe the sealing edges with a damp cloth. Then, close the jars. Also, adjust the bands/rings to seal and prevent any leakage.

Place the jars in a dry and dark place. Allow to cool.

Store in your refrigerator and use it within 10 days.

Nutrition: 139 kCal

CHAPTER 4:

Water Bath Recipes: Jams

Strawberry Jam
Preparation Time: 10 minutes
Cooking Time: 30 minutes
Servings: 12
Ingredients:

      10 cups strawberries, Clean & remove stems
      1.75 oz. pectin
      4 cups sugar
      ¼ cup tequila
      1 lime juice
      1 tsp. salt

Directions:
Add strawberries into the large pot and mash strawberries using a masher.
Add lime juice and salt and stir well.
Mix pectin with ¼ cup of sugar and sprinkle over berries. Bring to boil and stir constantly.
Remove pot from heat. Stir in tequila.
Ladle jam into the clean jar. Leave ½-inch headspace. Remove air bubbles.
Seal jars and set them in a boiling water bath for 10 minutes.
After this, remove jars from the water bath and let them cool.
Label and store.
Nutrition: 302 kCal

Strawberry Chia Jam
Preparation Time: 10 minutes
Cooking Time: 35 minutes
Servings: 8
Ingredients:
>   2 lbs. strawberries, hulled
>   1 ½ tbsp fresh lemon juice
>   2 tbsp chia seeds
>   ¼ cup maple syrup

Directions:
Add strawberries and maple syrup into the saucepan and cook over medium heat. After 5 minutes mash the strawberries using a masher.
Add lemon juice and also chia seeds and stir well. Turn heat to medium-low and cook for a few minutes, about 30 minutes or until jam is thickened.
Remove pan from heat then let it cool.
Pour jam in a clean jar. Seal the jar and store it in the refrigerator.
Nutrition:71kCal

Orange Jam
Preparation Time: 10 minutes
Cooking Time: 40 minutes
Servings: 6
Ingredients:
>   5 cups orange puree
>   1 cinnamon sticks
>   1-star anise
>   1 whole clove
>   1 cup sugar

Directions:
Add orange puree, spices, and sugar into the saucepan and simmer over medium heat for 20-30 minutes or until jam is thickened.
Remove pan from heat.
Ladle jam into the clean jar. Leave ½-inch headspace. Remove air bubbles.
Seal jars and set it in a boiling water bath for 10 minutes.
After, remove jars from the water bath and let it cool.
Label and store.
Nutrition:242kCal

Apricot Jam

Preparation Time: 10 minutes
Cooking Time: 40 minutes
Servings: 6
Ingredients:

> 2 lbs. apricots, wash, cut in half & pitted
> 4 tbsp lemon juice
> 1 cup sugar
> 1/2 cup water

Directions:
Add apricots and water in a saucepan and simmer over medium-low heat for 10 minutes. Stir constantly.
Add the lemon juice and sugar and stir well and simmer for 40 minutes or until apricots mixture thickens.
Remove saucepan from heat.
Ladle jam in clean and hot jars. Leave 1/4-inch headspace.
Seal jars. Set it in a water bath canner for 10 minutes.
After, remove the jars from the water bath and let it cool.
Check seals of jars. Label and store.
Nutrition: 201 kCal

Blueberry Chia Jam

Preparation Time: 10 minutes
Cooking Time: 18 minutes
Servings: 8
Ingredients:

> 3 cups blueberries
> 3 tbsp maple syrup
> 3 tbsp chia seeds

Directions:
Add blueberries and maple syrup into the saucepan and bring to boil over medium-low heat. Cover and cook for 3-5 minutes.
Using masher crush the berries until getting desired consistency.
Stiring chia seeds then it turns heat to low. Stir frequently and cook for 10-13 minutes or until jam thickens.
After doing this, remove the pan from the heat and then let it cool.
Pour jam in a clean jar. Seal jar and instantly store in the refrigerator for up to 2 weeks.
Nutrition: 64 kCal

Mixed Berry Jam

Preparation Time: 10 minutes
Cooking Time: 40 minutes
Servings: 12
Ingredients:

> 3 cups strawberries
> 2 1/2 cups blackberries
> 2 1/2 cups blueberries
> 1 tbsp fresh lemon juice
> 7 cups sugar
> 1.75 oz. fruit pectin

Directions:

Add all berries in a saucepan and cook over medium-low heat until berries are softened. Mashed berries using a masher. In a cup, mix together pectin, 2 cups of sugar and pectin and add into the berry mixture and boil over high heat. Add the remaining sugar and boil for 1 minute. Stir constantly. Remove saucepan from heat.

Ladle jam into the jars. Leave 1/2-inch headspace.

Seal jars with lids. Set it in a water bath canner for 10 minutes.

After, remove jars from the water bath and let it cool.

Check seals of jars. Label and store.

Nutrition: 479 kCal

Peach Jam

Preparation Time: 10 minutes
Cooking Time: 30 minutes
Servings: 14
Ingredients:

> 4 lbs. peaches, peel, pitted & chopped
> 2 tbsp lemon juice
> 1/2 tsp. nutmeg
> 2 1/2 cups sugar

Directions:

Add peaches into the blender and blend until get the desired consistency.

Add peaches, nutmeg, sugar, and lemon juice into a saucepan and cook over medium heat. Stir to dissolve sugar.

Bring it to boil and stir constantly until the jam is thickened.

Remove saucepan from heat and let stand for 10 minutes.

Pour jam in clean and warm jars. Seal jars with lids. Set it in the water bath canner for 10 minutes.

After, remove jars from the water bath and let it cool. Check seals of jars. Label and store.

Nutrition: 150 kCal

Mango Jam
Preparation Time: 10 minutes
Cooking Time: 40 minutes
Servings: 8
Ingredients:
>   4 cups mango, peel & chopped
>   3 cups sugar
>   1/2 cup lemon juice

Directions:
First, add all the asked ingredients in a saucepan and bring to boil over medium-high heat. Stir frequently.
Boil the jam for 20 minutes or until thickens.
Once the jam is thickened then remove the saucepan from heat.
Ladle jam into the jars. Leave 1/4-inch headspace.
Seal jars. Set it in a water bath canner for 10 minutes.
After, remove jars from the water bath and let it cool.
Check seals of jars. Label and store.
Nutrition: 295 kCal

Black Raspberry Jam
Preparation Time: 10 minutes
Cooking Time: 60 minutes
Servings: 8
Ingredients:
>   1 lb. black raspberries
>   1 3/4 cups granulated sugar
>   1 1/2 tbsp lemon juice

Directions:
Add berries, lemon juice, and sugar in a saucepan and cook over medium heat. Mash berries and stir occasionally.
Once berries release their juices then set heat to high and cook berries until thicken.
Cook over high heat for around 40 minutes or until getting gel consistency.
Once get gel consistency then remove the pan from heat.
Ladle jam in clean and hot jars. Leave 1/4-inch headspace.
Seal jars. Set it in a water bath canner for 20 minutes.
After, remove jars from the water bath and let it cool.
Check seals of jars. Label and store.
Nutrition: 205 kCal

Plum Jam
Preparation Time: 10 minutes
Cooking Time: 50 minutes
Servings: 12
Ingredients:
- 3 lbs. plums, halved, pitted & quartered
- 3 cups sugar
- 1/2 cup lemon juice
- 1/2 cup water

Directions:
First, add all ingredients in a saucepan and bring to a boil. Stir until sugar is dissolved.
Stir for 15-20 minutes or until getting gel consistency.
Remove pan from heat.
Ladle jam into the clean and hot jars.
Seal jars. Set it in a water bath canner for 10 minutes.
After, remove jars from the water bath and let it cool.
Check seals of jars. Label and store.
Nutrition:180 kCal

Grapefruit Jam
Preparation Time: 10 minutes
Cooking Time: 45 minutes
Servings: 14
Ingredients:
- 9 grapefruits, Peel and separate segments
- 3 1/2 cups sugar

Directions:
Add grapefruit segments into the blender and blend until smooth.
Add blended grapefruit mixture and sugar in a pot and simmer until sugar is dissolved.
Use high-heat to bring to boil.
Cook grapefruit mixture until reaches a temp. 220 F.
Remove pot from heat.
Ladle jam in clean jars. Seal jars with lids.
Set it in a water bath canner for 10 minutes.
After, remove jars from the water bath and let it cool.
Check seals of jars. Label and store.
Nutrition:215 kCal

WATER BATH CANNING AND PRESERVING

Carrot Jam
Preparation Time: 10 minutes
Cooking Time: 15 minutes
Servings: 30
Ingredients:

> 1 1/2 lbs. carrots, peel and grate 2 oz. carrots
> 2 1/3 cup sugar
> 2 lemon juice

Directions:
Peel and chop remaining carrots.
Add carrots in the saucepan and pour enough water to cover carrots. Cook carrots until soften.
Drain the carrots well and puree with a blender.
Add grated carrot, carrot puree, and sugar in a large saucepan and bring to boil for 5 minutes.
Pull outthe saucepan from the heat and let it cool for 10 minutes. Stir in lemon juice.
Pour jam into the clean jars and seal jars with lids. Label and store.
Nutrition:65 kCal

Pearl Jam
Preparation Time: 10 minutes
Cooking Time: 30 minutes
Servings: 10
Ingredients:

> 5 pears, peeled, cored, and also cut into chunks
> 1/2 cup brown sugar
> 1 tbsp ginger, grated
> 1 lemon juice

Directions:
Add pears, lemon juice, sugar, and ginger to the large saucepan and bring to boil over medium-high heat.
Reduce heat and cook the jam for 10-15 minutes or until thickened.
Ladle jam into the clean jars. Leave 1/4-inch headspace.
Seal jar with a lid. Set it in a water bath canner for 10 minutes.
After, remove jars from the water bath and let it cool.
Check seals of jars. Label and store.
Nutrition:90 kCal

CHAPTER 5:

Water Bath Recipes: Salsas

Corn Relish
Preparation Time: 20 minutes
Cooking Time: 50 minutes
Servings: 3-4 pints
Ingredients:

   2 teaspoons mustard seeds
   1/2 teaspoon turmeric
   1/2 teaspoon ground cumin
   1 large cucumber, seeded, peeled, roughly chopped
   1 1/2 cups apple cider vinegar, 5% acidity
   2 cups of onions, chopped
   1 red bell peppers, chopped and seeded
   4 cups corn kernels
   2 plum or Roma tomatoes, diced
   1 red or green serrano chili peppers, seeded and minced

1 1/4 cups sugar

2 tablespoons kosher salt

1/2 teaspoon black pepper

Directions:

Pulse cucumbers, onions, bell peppers: Working per batch if needed, pulse the cucumbers, onions, and bell peppers in a food processor only 3 or 4 pulses, so they are as yet discernable from one another, not puréed.

Combine with remaining ingredients, simmer 25 minutes: Place mixture in a medium-sized (4 to 6-quart), thick-bottomed pot. Add the corn, tomatoes, serranochilies, sugar, salt, pepper, vinegar, turmeric, mustard seed, and ground cumin. Bring to a boil. Reduce heat to a simmer. Cover and cook for 25 minutes.

Scoop into jars: Spoon the corn relish into clean jars and seal, will last for 4-6 weeks refrigerated.

Nutrition: 354 kCal

Salsa Verde

Preparation Time: 20 minutes

Cooking Time: 10 minutes

Servings: 3 pints

Ingredients:

12 medium green tomatoes, cored, peeled and diced

6 to 8 jalapenos, seeded and minced

2 large red onion, diced

1 teaspoon minced garlic

½ cup fresh lime juice

½ cup fresh chopped cilantro

1 ½ teaspoons ground cumin

1 teaspoon dried oregano

Salt and pepper

Directions:

Prepare the needed equipment: your water bath canner as well as your lids and bands.

Combine the tomatoes, jalapenos, onion, garlic and lime juice in a bigsaucepan.

Cover and bring to a boil then stir in the remaining ingredients.

Reduce heat and simmer for 5 minutes then spoon the mixture into your jars, leaving about ½-inch bands of headspace.

Clean the rims, add the lid and seal with a metal band then place the jars in the water bath canner and bring the water to boil.

Process the jars for 20 minutes then remove the jars and wipe them dry.

Place these jars on a canning rack and cool for 24 hours before storing.

Nutrition: 276 kCal

Simple Salsa

Preparation Time: 20
minutes **Cooking Time:** 60
minutes **Servings:** 3 pints
Ingredients:

> 4 cups slicing tomatoes, cored and chopped
> 2 cups green chilies, seeded and chopped
> ¾ cup onions, chopped
> ½ cup jalapeno peppers, seeded and chopped
> 4 garlic cloves, chopped
> 1 teaspoon ground cumin
> 1 tablespoon cilantro
> 1 tablespoon oregano
> 2 cups distilled white vinegar
> 1 ½ teaspoons table salt

Directions:

Place all the said ingredients above in a large pot. Place the pot on the stove and immediately bring to a rolling boil while stirring constantly to prevent burning. Minimize the heat a bit and let the mixture simmer for about 20 minutes. Stir frequently. Divide the salsa among 4 jars. Make sure to leave about ½-inch of space at the top of each jar. Place the lids on the jars andprocess using the water bath canning method for 25 to 35 minutes.
Nutrition:225 kCal

Pineapple Chipotle

Preparation Time: 20 minutes
Cooking Time: 10 minutes
Servings: 3 pints
Ingredients:

> 4 Cup seeded papaya
> 2 Cup chopped or cubed pineapples
> 1 Cup raisins
> 1 Cup lemon juice
> ½ Cup lime juice
> ½ Cup pineapple juice
> ½ Cup Anaheim peppers
> 2 Tablespoons chopped onions
> 2 Tablespoons chopped cilantro
> 2 Tablespoons brown sugar

Directions:

Add together all 10 ingredients together in a saucepan and bring to a bowl, but you need to stir constantly. Reduce to a steady simmer and let thicken but stirring constantly. Add to the canning jars and seal.
Nutrition: 233 kCal

Mango Salsa

Preparation Time: 20 minutes
Cooking Time: 10 minutes
Servings: 3 pints
Ingredients:

- ½ cup Water
- 1 ¼ cup Cider vinegar, 5%
- 2 teaspoons Ginger, chopped
- 1 ½ cups Red bell pepper, diced
- 1/2 teaspoon Red pepper flakes, crushed
- 6 cups Mango, unripe, diced
- 1/2 cup Yellow onion, chopped
- 2 teaspoons Garlic, chopped
- 1 cup Brown sugar

Directions:

Thoroughly wash the mangoes and the rest of the produce.

Peel the mangoes before chopping in half-inch cubes.

Chop the yellow onion into fine bits and dice the red bell pepper in half-inch strips. Place this in a stock pot or Dutch oven. Add all other ingredients, stir to combine, and heat over high heat.

Once the mixture is boiling, give it a good stir to dissolve the sugar. Turn the heat down to medium and allow the mixture to simmer for about five minutes.

Pour the hot salsa into clean and hot Mason jars, leaving half an inch of headspace in each jar. Pour the hot liquid into it to fill each jar half an inch from the rim.

Take out any air bubbles before securing the jar lids. Place in the water bath and process for ten minutes.

Nutrition: 299 kCal

Tomatillo Salsa

Preparation Time: 20 minutes
Cooking Time: 10 minutes
Servings: 2 1/2 pints
Ingredients:

- 1 ½ pounds tomatillos, husked and rinsed
- 1 to 2 medium jalapeños, stemmed (note: spiciness will depend on the heat of actual peppers used)
- ½ cup chopped white onion
- 1 to 2 juiced medium limes
- ½ to 1 teaspoon salt
- ¼ cup packed fresh cilantro leaves

Directions:

Preheat the broiler with a rack around 4 inches below the source of heat. Place the tomatillos and jalapeños on a rimmed baking sheet and broil until they're blackened in spots, about 5 minutes.

Remove the baking sheet from the oven, slowly flip over the tomatillos and peppers using tongs and broil for around 4 to 6 more minutes, until the tomatillos are splotchy-black and blistered.

After a while, in a food processor or blender, join the cleaved onion, cilantro, 2 tablespoons lime juice and ½ teaspoon salt. When the tomatillos are out of the broiler, cautiously move the hot tomatillos, peppers and all of their juices into the blender or food processor.

After this, pulse until the mixture is almost smooth and there are no big chunks of tomatillo that remain. Scrape down the sides as necessary then season with additional lime juice and salt, if desired.

The salsa will be thinner in the beginning, but will eventually thicken up following a couple of hours in the fridge, because of the normally occurring pectin in the tomatillos.

Nutrition: 180 kCal

Zesty Salsa
Preparation Time: 20 minutes
Cooking Time: 10 minutes
Servings: 6 pints
Ingredients:

> 10 cups roughly chopped tomatoes
> 1 (6 ounces) can tomato paste
> 2 1/2 cups hot peppers, chopped, seeded
> 5 cups chopped and seeded bell peppers
> 5 cups chopped onions
> 1 1/4 cups cider vinegar
> 3 garlic cloves, minced
> 2 tablespoons cilantro, minced
> 3 teaspoons salt

Directions:
Combine all the said ingredients except for the tomato paste in a large sauce pot. Simmer until desired thickness.
Stir in tomato paste.
Ladle hot salsa into the pre-sterilized hot jars leaving 1/4 inch head-space.
Process this in a hot water bath for 10 minutes.
Nutrition: 142 kCal

Green Salsa
Preparation Time: 20 minutes
Cooking Time: 10 minutes
Servings: 3 pints
Ingredients:

> 7 Cups chopped green tomatoes
> 3 Cups chopped jalapenos
> 2 Cups chopped red onions
> 2 Teaspoons minced garlic
> ½ Cups lime juice
> ½ Cups chopped cilantro
> 2 teaspoon ground cumin

Directions:
Combine all the vegetables and the garlic and lime in a saucepan and boil then simmer for 5 minutes, spoon salsa into canning jars and leave ¼" at the top for the canning process.
Nutrition:133kCal

Corn & Cherry Tomato Salsa

Preparation Time: 20 minutes
Cooking Time: 10 minutes
Servings: 6 pints
Ingredients:

> ½ cup chopped fresh cilantro
> 1 cup red onion, chopped
> 5 pounds cherry tomatoes, roughly chopped
> 2 jalapeño peppers, seeded and minced
> 2 cups corn kernels (may be fresh or frozen thawed)
> ½ cup fresh lime juice (3 large or 4 medium limes)
> 2 teaspoons salt
> 1 teaspoon chipotle chili powder, optional

Directions:

Set up the bubbling water canner. Warm the containers in stewing water until they're prepared for use. Do not boil. Wash the tops in warm lathery water and put them aside with the groups.

Bring all the said ingredients to a boil in huge treated steel or plated pan. Diminish the warmth and stew for 5 to 10 minutes, blending sporadically.

Scoop the hot salsa into a hot container, leaving ½-inch of headspace. Eliminate the air bubbles. Wipe the container edge clean. Focus the top on the container. Apply the band and change in accordance with fingertip-tight. Spot the container in the bubbling water canner. Rehash until all the containers are filled.

Process the used jars in a water bathfor 15 minutes, adjusting depending on the altitude. Turn off the heat, then remove the lid, and then let the jars stand for at least 5 minutes. Remove the jars and let them cool.

Nutrition: 311 kCal

Classic Fiesta Salsa

Preparation Time: 20 minutes
Cooking Time: 1 ½ hours
Servings: 32
Ingredients:

> 4 ½ Cups of Tomatoes, diced
> 3 Tablespoons of Vinegar, White
> ¼ Cup of Salsa

Directions:
First and foremost, combine your diced tomatoes, vinegar and favorite kind of salsa in a large sized saucepan placed over medium heat. Cook your mixture until boiling. Once your mixture is boiling reduce the heat to low and then allow to simmer for the next 5 minutes. Remove from heat and permit to cool totally.
Pour your mixture into your canning jars and seal with your lids.
Boil your jars in some boiling water for the next 10 minutes. Remove and make sure to allow to cool slightly before placing it into your fridge. Use whenever you are ready.
Nutrition: 152 kCal

Fresh Tomato Salsa

Preparation Time: 20 minutes
Cooking Time: 30 minutes
Servings: 4 pints
Ingredients:

> 4 lbs. fresh chopped tomatoes
> 2 large green peppers, cored and chopped
> 2 large yellow onions, chopped
> 1 large jalapeno, seeded and minced
> 2 tablespoons fresh chopped cilantro
> 1 tablespoon minced garlic
> 2 teaspoons canning salt
> 1/3 cup distilled white vinegar

Directions:
Prepare your water bath canner and your jars.
Combine all of the said ingredients in a large saucepan and bring to a boil.
Diminish the heat and then simmer the salsa for 5 minutes.
Spoon the salsa into your prepared jars, leaving about ½ inch of headspace.
Clean the jars and add them to the water bath canner according to the step-by-step guide. Process the jars for 35 minutes then cool according to the step-by-step guide.
Nutrition: 162 kCal

CHAPTER 6:

Pressure Canning Recipes: Legumes

Black Bean Salad
Preparation Time: 10 minutes
Cooking Time: 20 minutes
Servings: 4-6
Ingredients:
1 box of black beans rinsed and drained 540 ml
1 cup drained corn kernels
1 diced green pepper
3 green onions, minced
2 c. tablespoon extra-virgin olive oil
1 tsp. table balsamic vinegar
Some sprigs of parsley or coriander.
Directions:
Using a bowl, combine all the ingredients and serve.
For softer green onions, let them marinate for a few minutes in balsamic vinegar then drain the excess vinegar before adding them to the rest of the ingredients.
NOTE See page 79 for instructions
Nutrition: 257 kCal

Cowboy Beans

Preparation Time: 2 hours
Cooking Time: 15 minutes
Servings: 6
Ingredients:

>   3 cans of baked beans (e.g. from Heinz)
>   1 can of kidney beans
>   2 onions diced
>   200 g bacon
>   4 tbsp maple syrup
>   10 tbsp BBQ sauce (for example BBQUE Original)
>   3 tbsp BBQ Rub (e.g. Magic Dust)

Directions:

1.   Put dried beans in a pot. Add 1 ½ litres (6 cups) of water. Boil 2 minutes, remove from heat and let stand for an hour, covered.
2.   Make your sauce flavouring mixture by mixing together everything from onion down to Kitchen Bouquet (if using) in a large microwave-safe bowl or jug; set aside.
3.   Drain the beans, discarding the soaking water.
4.   Put beans in a large pot, add 2 bay leaves, cover with 2 to 5 cm (1 to 2 inches) of water, bring to a full boil, boil for a minute or two, then turn off the heat. Don't boil much longer or you will end up with mooshy beans at the end of everything.
5.   Drain the beans in a way that will preserve the water this time. (See suggestions in notes.) Discard the 2 bay leaves.
6.   Take 750 ml (3 cups / 24 oz) of that reserved water. Add it to the sauce flavouring mixture you had set aside, cover that bowl or large jug and zap in microwave for 5 minutes to make a sauce.
7.   Take the sauce out of the microwave, stir (mind the surge). Set aside.
8.   The headspace on this recipe is 3 cm (1 inch) per jar. Bearing that in mind and taking that into account, fill each jar (minus that reserved headspace in your mind) ¾ full of plain beans.
9.   Fill up the remaining ¼ of each jar with sauce, leaving still the 3 cm (1 inch) headspace.
10.   At this point, the USDA notes that you may "add a ¾-inch (2 cm) cube of pork, ham, or bacon to each jar, if desired."
11.   Add additional water to jars from the reserved bean stock if you run short on sauce.
12.   Debubble, then top up with a bit more sauce or bean stock as needed to maintain the 2 cm (1 inch) headspace.
13.   So to recap, a jar will 3 cm (1 inch) blank headspace at the top. Of the remaining jar space below that, ¾ of that space will be plain beans, then ¼ plain sauce.
14.   Debubble, adjust headspace.
15.   Wipe jar rims.
16.   Put lids on.
17.   Processing pressure: based on your location (adjust pressure for your altitude when over 300 metres / 1000 feet)
18.   Processing time: quarter-litre (½ US pint / 250 ml) OR half-litre (1 US pint): 65 minutes. 1 litre (1 US quart): 75 minutes.

Nutrition: 367 kCal

Bread and Bean Chard Soup

Preparation Time: 15 minutes
Cooking Time: 50 minutes
Servings: 6-7
Ingredients:

      2 shallots
      2 cloves of garlic
      1 tbsp thyme
      6 slice (s) of bacon
      100 g bread (stale, cut into rough cubes)
      100 g beans
      10 fisoles (green)
      1 Swiss chard
      800 ml vegetable soup
      2 tomatoes
      2 tbsp balsamic vinegar
      1 bunch of basil
      Salt
      Pepper
      Olive oil

Directions:

Soak the beans in the water a day before, boil in plenty of water until soft, drain and continue to use for the soup.

Place the bacon on a baking sheet and fry until crispy at 160 ° C for about 14 minutes.

Peel the shallots and cloves of garlic and cut them into fine cubes. Cut the biscuits and chard into rough pieces, remove the core from the tomatoes and cut them into small cubes.

Fry the shallots, garlic, chard, and fisoles in a wide saucepan and pour on the soup. Approx. simmer for 10 minutes, and then add the tomatoes, the remaining beans, and the thyme. Season with salt, pepper, and vinegar.

Shortly before serving, mix the bread with the soup and garnish with fresh basil and bacon.

NOTE See page 79 for instructions

Nutrition: 212 kCal

Quinoa and Black Beans
Preparation Time: 15 minutes
Cooking Time: 35 minutes
Servings: 8
Ingredients:

>1 tsp. vegetable oil
>1 onion, chopped
>3 pieces of chopped garlic
>Quinoa ¾ cup
>Vegetable soup 1 1 cup
>1 teaspoon of ground cumin
>approx.teaspoon salt and black pepper
>1 cup of frozen corn
>2 cans of black beans
>½ cup of freshly chopped coriander

Directions:
Firstly, heat the oil over medium heat in a saucepan; cook and stir until lightly browned, around 10 minutes.

Cover with vegetable broth; season with cumin, cayenne pepper, salt, and pepper. Bring to boil the mixture. Cover, reduce heat, and cook until the quinoa is tender and broth absorbed, about 20 minutes.

Drop frozen corn into the saucepan and simmer until heated through, about 5 minutes; mix in black beans and cilantro.

Nutrition: 1660 kCal

NOTE See page 79 for instructions

Vegan Green Hummus

Preparation Time: 1 hour
Cooking Time: 5 minutes
Servings: 3
Ingredients:

> 1 bunch parsley
> 1 bunch basil
> 3rd spring onions
> 240 g cooked chickpeas (home-cooked or canned)
> Juice of ½ lemon
> 2 tbsp Tahin (Sesammus)
> 5 tbsp olive oil
> salt
> pepper

Directions:

Wash the parsley and basil and shake well until dry. Pluck the leaves and chop them roughly. Clean, wash and roughly cut the spring onions into pieces.

Put herbs and spring onions with chickpeas, lemon juice, tahini and oil in a tall mixing beaker and puree everything with a hand blender. Season the hummus with salt and with pepper and let it sit for 1 hour before serving.

Nutrition: 142 kCal

Red Rice and Beans

Preparation Time: 20 minutes
Cooking Time: 2 hours
Servings: 6-8
Ingredients:

> 200 g dried red beans
> 2 bay leaves
> 250 g long grain rice
> pepper
> salt

Directions:

Soak the beans in about 1/2 liter of cold water overnight.

Put the beans in a saucepan the day after, cover with water and cook with laurel for 30 minutes to 2 hours on mild heat. Cook the rice according to the package instructions. Drain the beans, mix with the rice, salt, and pepper. Serve the rice with beans the veal cutlets.

NOTE See page 79 for instructions

Nutrition: 142 kCal

Tuscan White Beans

Preparation Time: 15 minutes
Cooking Time: 1 hour and 30 minutes
Servings: 4
Ingredients:

> 300 g dried white beans
> 2 l instant vegetable broth
> 1 sprig (s) of fresh rosemary
> 0.5 bunch of fresh thyme
> 1 bunch of flat-leaf parsley
> 1 clove (s) of fresh garlic
> 100 ml of olive oil plus some salt and pepper
> 1 tbsp grated lemon zest (untreated)
> 3 tsp. lemon juice, freshly squeezed

Directions:

Soak white beans overnight, and then cook open in the vegetable broth for 1.5 hours.

Chop the herbs, peel, and press the garlic. Carefully heat both in olive oil. Put the beans dripping wet in the herb oil, bring to the boil and season with salt, pepper, lemon zest, and lemon juice.

Nutrition: 245 kCal

Slow Cooker Chicken Chili

Preparation Time: 10 minutes
Cooking Time: 8 hours
Servings: 8
Ingredients:

> 2 cans (19 oz. or 540 ml each) mixed beans, rinsed
> 2 cups of salsa
> 1 can (14 oz. or 398 ml) diced tomatoes without added salt, undrained
> 2 c. tablespoon chili powder
> 1 1/2 lb. (or 675 g) boneless chicken thighs, cut into small pieces
> 1 onion, chopped
> 1 cup of frozen corn
> 1 cup Light Cracker Barrel Shredded Tex Mex Cheese

Directions:

Combine the first four ingredients mentioned above in the slow cooker; cover with chicken, onion, and corn. (Do not mix.) Cover.

On a low heat, cook the mixture for around 8 hours (or high for 4 to 5 hours). Toss and garnish with cheese before serving.

NOTE See page 79 for instructions

Nutrition: 313 kCal

CHAPTER 7:

Pressure Canning Recipes: Vegetables and Tomatoes

Pressure Canned Potatoes

Preparation Time: 35 minutes
Cooking Time: 40 minutes
Servings: 7-quart jars
Ingredients:

>6 lb. white potatoes
>Canning salt

Directions:

Wash the jars thoroughly then place them in a cold oven. Heat it to 250°F.

Meanwhile, bring water in a pot to boil. Also, add 4 inches of water in the pressure canner and place it over medium heat.

Peel the potatoes and cut them into 2 inches pieces.

Add a tablespoon of salt in each jar then fill with potatoes leaving 1-inch headspace. Pour the boiling water into each jar then use a canning knife to remove the air bubbles from the jars.

Wipe the jar rims and then place the lids and rings on the jars. After which, place the jars in the pressure canner and secure the lid according to the manufacture instructions.

Process the jars at 10 pounds for 40 minutes and 35 minutes for pit jars.

Turn off the heat and let the canner depressurize before removing the jars. Place the jars on a towel undisturbed for 24 hours.

Store in a cool dry place.

Nutrition: 108kCal

Pressure Canned Corn

Preparation Time: 35 minutes
Cooking Time: 55 minutes
Servings: 5 quart jars
Ingredients:
2lb Fresh corn
Water
Salt
Directions:
Cut off the corn from its cob and bring water to boil.
Pack the corn kernels in the jars and leave a 1-inch headspace. Add a half tablespoon of salt to each jar then add the boiled water to cover the corn.
Remove any air bubbles and add more water if necessary.
Wipe the rims and immediatelyplace the lids and rings on the jars. Transfer the jars to the pressure canner and process them at 10 pounds pressure for 55 minutes.
Let the canner depressurize before removing the jars. Store in a cool dry place.
Nutrition:177 kCal

Pressure Canned Carrots

Preparation Time: 35 minutes
Cooking Time:40 minutes
Servings: 7-quart jars
Ingredients:
2-1/2 lb. Carrots
Salt
Water
Directions:
Wash the carrots and trim them. Peel the carrots and wash them again if you desire.
Slice the carrots into pieces of your liking.
Pack the carrots in the jars leaving 1-inch headspace. Add a 1/2 tablespoon of salt to each jar then add boiling water to each jar.
Get rid of the air bubbles and add more hot water if necessary. Wipe the jar rims using a clean damp towel, then place the lids on the jars.
After which, place the jars in the pressure canner and process them for 25 minutes at 10 pounds pressure.
Let the canner rest and depressurize before removing the jar.
Nutrition:27 kCal

Pressure Canned Asparagus
Preparation Time: 35 minutes
Cooking Time: 30 minutes
Servings: 9-quart jars
Ingredients:
10 lb. asparagus
Canning salt
Boiling water
Directions:
First, bring the water to boil using a pot over high heat.
Trim the asparagus such that they fit in the jars. Pack them in the jars, add 1/2 tablespoon salt and the boiling water leaving 1-inch headspace. Wipe the jar rims, place the lids, place the rings, and use hands to tighten. After which, put the jars in the pressure canner and process at 10 pounds for a minimum of 30 minutes for pints and at least 40 minutes for quarts.
Allow the pressure canner to depressurize before removing the jars.
Nutrition: 20 kCal

Pressure Canned Plain Beets
Preparation Time: 35 minutes
Cooking Time: 40 minutes
Servings: 3-quart jars
Ingredients:
1 lb. Beets
Water
Pickling salt
Directions:
Trim the tops of the beets leaving an inch long top. Also, leave the roots on the beets.
Wash the beets thoroughly with clean water then put them in a pot.
Cover the beets with water and bring to boil for 15-25 minutes or until the skin can come out easily.
Remove the beets from hot water and let them cool a little bit such that you can hold them. They should be at least warm when being put in the jar.
Trim the remaining stem and roots then peel the beets.
Slice the beets into large slices leaving the small ones whole. Put the beets in jars and leave a 1-inch headspace.
Add a half tablespoon of salt in each jar then add boiling water in each jar.
Remove any bubbles in the jar then wipe the rims with a clean piece of cloth.
Put on the lids and the rings. Process the jars at 10 pounds for 30 minutes.
Let the pressure canner depressurize to zero before removing the jars.
Nutrition: 58 kCal

Canned Pumpkin

Preparation Time: 35 minutes
Cooking Time: 40 minutes
Servings: 3quart jars
Ingredients:
1 lb. Pie pumpkins
Water
Directions:
Start by cutting out the stem as if you want to use the pumpkin to curve, then cut it into 4 equal wedges.
Scrap out the seeds then use a knife to peel the pumpkin. Slice the pumpkin into 1-inch cubes.
After this, place the pumpkin cubes in a large pot and water until the pumpkin is just covered.
Bring the pumpkin and water to boil for 2 minutes. Carefully transfer the pumpkin pieces into jars making sure you avoid smashing them.
Fill each jar with the cooking liquid leaving 1-inch headspace. Wipe the jar rims with a clean damp piece of cloth. After which, place the lids and rings on the jars and place them in the pressure canner. Process the jars at 15 pounds pressure for 90 minutes for quart jars and for 55 minutes for pint jars.
Wait until the pressure canner has depressurized to zero before removing the jars.
Nutrition: 49 kCal

Pressure Canned Hot peppers

Preparation Time: 35 minutes
Cooking Time: 45 minutes
Servings: 2-pint jars
Ingredients:
2 lb. hot peppers
Salt
Directions:
Wear rubber gloves on your hands to avoid a burning sensation.
Sort the peppers and select the fresh and firm ones for maximum results.
Wash the hot peppers and place them on a lined baking sheet in a single layer.
Broil in the broiler for 5-10 minutes making sure you flip over once.
Transfer the hot pepper to a zip lock bag and seal tightly. Let rest for 10 minutes then remove them from the bag. Rub off as much peppers skin as much as possible.
Trim the tops off, scrape out the seeds, then cut the peppers into two or into sizes that will fit in the jar. Pac the peppers in the jars then add a half tablespoon of salt to each jar. Add boil water to each bar leaving 1-inch headspace. Wipe the rims, close the lids and place the rings in place.
Process the jars for 35 minutes at 10 pounds pressure.
Wait for the scanner to depressurize before removing the jars out.
Nutrition: 6kCal

Pressure Canned Sweet peppers

Preparation Time: 35 minutes
Cooking Time: 35 minutes
Servings: 2 pint jars
Ingredients:
2 lb. sweet bell peppers
Salt
Directions:
Thoroughly wash the sweet bell peppers then cut them into quarters.

Place the peppers in a pot covered with water and bring to boil for 3 minutes.

Transfer the peppers into the pint jars then add a quarter tablespoon of salt in each jar.

Ladle the cooking liquid in each jar leaving 1-inch headspace. Make sure to wipe the rims and place the lids and rings.

After which, place the jars in the pressure canner and process for 35 minutes at 10 pounds pressure.

Let the pressure canner depressurize before removing the jars.

Nutrition: 46 kCal

Pressure Canned Sweet Potatoes

Preparation Time: 35 minutes
Cooking Time: 40 minutes
Servings: 10-quart jars
Ingredients:
10 lb. sweet potatoes
Water
1-1/2 cup sugar
Directions:
Add the whole sweet potatoes into a stockpot, then add water until they are covered. Bring to boil for 15 minutes.

Remove the sweet potatoes from water and let them cool so that they are easy to peel.

Cut them into large chunks then pack them in the clean jars leaving a half-inch headspace.

Bring it to boil 3 cups of water and add 1-1/2 cups of brown sugar until the sugar has dissolved.

Add boiled water to some of the jars and simple brown sugar syrup to others but maintain the headspace. Remove the bubble and add more hot water if necessary.

Wipe the jar rims then palace the lids and rings on. After which, place the jars in the canner and process for at 10 pounds for 90 minutes for quart jars and 65 minutes for pint jars.

Let the pressure drop so that you can remove the jars from the canner.

Nutrition: 86 kCal

Pressure Canned Broccoli

Preparation Time: 35 minutes
Cooking Time: 33 minutes
Servings: 4-pint jars
Ingredients:
4 lb. fresh broccoli
Canning salt
Water
Directions:
Soak then thoroughly wash the broccoli to remove all the dirt that could be in the head.
Cut the head into 2-inch pieces and discard the stems. You can also can the stems if you desire.
Place the broccoli in boiling water and let it boil for 3 minutes.
Use a slotted spoon to pack the broccoli in sterilized jars then add the hot water in each jar leaving 1-inch headspace. Release any air bubbles in each jar and add the water if necessary.
Add 1 tablespoon of canning salt to each jar then wipe the rims with a clean towel. Place the lids and rings then transfer the jars to the pressure canner.
Process the jars at 10 pounds for 30 minutes. Let the canner depressurize before removing the jars.
Let the jars rest overnight to store them in a cool dry place.
Nutrition: 8 kCal

Canned Kale

Preparation Time: 35 minutes
Cooking Time: 80 minutes
Servings: 5-pint jars
Ingredients:
10 lb. Kale
Water
Directions:
Chop the kale into bite-size pieces then remove all the hard stems and yellow parts of the kale.
Rinse the kale to get rid of any dirt then add it to the stockpot. Cover the kale with water.
Bring the water to boil until the kale has wilted nicely.
Use a slotted spoon to fill the jars with kale then add 1/2 tablespoon salt in each jar. Add the cooking liquid and leave a 1-inch headspace.
Remove any air bubble and add more cooking liquid if necessary. Wipe the rims and also place the lids and rings on the jars.
Process the jars at 10-11 pounds of pressure for 70 minutes. Turn off the heat and let the canner cool before using a jar lifer to remove the jars.
Let rest for 24 hours undisturbed before storing them in a cool dry place.
Nutrition: 85 kCal

Canning Turnips

Preparation Time: 35 minutes
Cooking Time: 40 minutes
Servings: 12-pint jars
Ingredients:
10 lb. turnips
Water
Directions:
Peel the turnips then dice them into small pieces
Add the turnips into a stockpot and add cold water until just covered. Drain the water to get rid of dirt and debris. Cover with water once more and bring them to boil over medium-high heat. Diminish heat and let simmer for 5 minutes.
Utilize a slotted spoon to transfer the hot turnips into sterilized jars. Fill the jar with the cooking liquid leaving 1-inch headspace. Add a half tablespoon of pickling salt.
Remove any air bubble and add the cooking liquid if necessary. Wipe the pint jars and place the lids and rings.
Load the jars into the pressure canner and process at 10 pounds for 30 minutes.
Allow the canner to depressurize to zero before removing the jars.
Nutrition: 36.4 kCal

Pressure Canned Caramelized Onions

Preparation Time: 35 minutes
Cooking Time: 10 hours and 70 minutes
Process Time: 70 minutes
Servings: 6-pint jars
Ingredients:
6 lb. Onions
2 stick butter
Water
Directions:
Peel the onions and also slice them into 1/4 inches slices.
Melt 1 stick of butter in the stockpot over high heat then add the diced onions.
Slice another stick of butter over the onions. Cook on high for an hour until the butter has melted and the onions were sweating a little bit.
Reduce the heat then let cook for 10 hours or overnight while stirring occasionally. The onions should be golden brown and well caramelized. Ladle the onions in the sterilized hot jars then remove any air bubbles. Also, wipe the jar rims with a damp clean cloth
Place the lid and rings on the jars and process them at 10 pounds pressure for 70 minutes. Remove the pressure canner from heat and let its pressure reduce to zero before removing the jars.
Nutrition: 178 kCal

Canned Fiddleheads

Preparation Time: 35 minutes
Cooking Time: 60 minutes
Servings: 1-pint jars
Ingredients:
2 cups fiddleheads
1/2 cup of water
1/2 cup white vinegar
1 tbsp salt
1/2 tbsp peppercorns
1/2 tbsp fennel
1/2 tbsp coriander
1 sprig thyme
3 garlic cloves
Directions:
Trim off the cut ends then boil the fiddleheads for 10 minutes in salted water.
Strain the fiddleheads and rinse them with clean water. Pack the fiddleheads in the jars and leave 1-inch headspace.
Add the spices directly into each jar on top of the fiddleheads.
Boil water, vinegar, and salt in a saucepan and pour over the fiddleheads.
Wipe the rims, then place the lids and the rings on the jars. After which, place the jars in the pressure canner and process at 10 pounds pressure for 10 minutes.
Nutrition:22 kCal

CHAPTER 8:

Pressure Canning Recipes: Conserves, Cheeses, Curds, and Butter

Hot Chili Pepper Butter

Preparation Time: 5 minutes
Cooking Time: 20 minutes
Servings: 8 pint jars
Ingredients:

   40 medium hot chili peppers (seeded, chopped fine)
   1 qtr. cider vinegar
   1 qtr. prepared yellow mustard
   6 cups sugar
   1 ¼ cups flour
   1 teaspoon salt
   1 ½ cups water

Directions:

Sterilize the jars.

Combine all the mentioned ingredients together in a pot and bring them
to boil. Boil for around 5 minutes, stirring continuously.

Turn-off the flame and skim-off any visible foam.

Ladle the mix immediately into the sterilized jars, leaving a quarter-inch of headspace. Get rid of any air bubbles and clean the rims.
Cover the jars with the lid and apply the bands making sure that it is tightened.
Submerge the jars within a prepared boiling water canner for 10 minutes.
Remove, allow to cool, and then label the jars.
Nutrition:93kCal

Lemony Curd

Preparation Time: 10 minutes
Cooking Time: 30 minutes
Servings:3 half-pint jars
Ingredients:

   ½ cup lemon juice
   6 egg yolks
   1 cup sugar
   1 stick of butter (chunked)
   4 tablespoon lemon zest

Directions:

Sterilize the jars.
Whisk the lemon juice, sugar and egg in a saucepan over medium flame and cook for 10-15 minutes, stirring continuously, ensuring that it does not boil.
Once the mixture thickens, add butter chunks a few at a time and stir the mix until melted.
Strain the mixture by using a fine mesh sieve and then whisk in the zest.
Turn-off the flame and skim-off any visible foam.
Ladle the mix immediately into the sterilized jars, leaving half-inch of headspace.
Get rid of any air bubbles and clean the rims.
Cover the jars with the lid and apply the bands making sure that it is tightened.
Submerge the jars within a prepared boiling water canner for 20 minutes.
Remove, allow to cool, and then label the jars.
Nutrition: 123 kCal

Banana & Pineapple Butter

Preparation Time: 10 minutes
Cooking Time: 30 minutes
Servings: 4 half-pint jars
Ingredients:

- 1 cup banana (mashed)
- 1 cup canned crushed pineapple (with juice)
- 2 tablespoon maraschino cherries (chopped)
- 2 teaspoon lemon juice (fresh)
- 3 ½ cups granulated sugar
- 3 oz. liquid pectin

Directions:

Sterilize the jars.

Combine all the mentioned ingredients except the pectin in a saucepan and bring to boil, stirring continuously.

Leave to boil for a minute.

Turn-off the flame, stir in the pectin for 5 minutes.

Skim-off any visible foam.

Ladle the mix immediately into the sterilized jars, leaving a quarter-inch of headspace.

Get rid of any air bubbles and clean the rims.

Cover the jars with the lid and apply the bands making sure that it is tightened.

Submerge the jars within a prepared boiling water canner for 5 minutes.

Remove, allow to cool, and then label the jars.

Nutrition: 116 kCal

Peachy Rum Conserve

Preparation Time: 15 minutes
Cooking Time: 45 minutes
Servings: 2 pint jars
Ingredients:

   3 tablespoons orange rind
   2/3 cup orange pulp
   1/2 cup maraschino cherries (chopped)
   1/2 cup light rum
   6 1/2 cups sugar
   2 cups peaches (peeled, pitted, chopped)
   1/2 teaspoon ginger
   1/4 teaspoon mace
   3/4 cup pineapple (crushed)
   3 tablespoons lemon juice
   1/2 teaspoon salt

Directions:

Sterilize the jars.

Mix together the orange pulp and orange rind in a pan and just cover with water, cooking until the rind is tender.

Place the rum container in hot water and place it aside.

Mix together the pineapple, peaches, lime juice and cherries in a pot along with the orange mix, then mix in the spices and sugar, stirring until the sugar dissolves.

Cook until it thickens, stirring frequently, then remove from heat and mix in the rum.

Skim-off any visible foam and ladle the mix immediately into the sterilized jars. Leave a quarter-inch of headspace, get rid of any air bubbles and clean the rims.

Cover the jars with the lid and apply the bands making sure that it is tightened.

Submerge the jars within a prepared boiling water canner for 15 minutes.

Remove, allow to cool, and then label the jars.

Nutrition: 220 kCal

Soft Cheese

Preparation Time: 10 minutes
Cooking Time: 40 minutes
Servings: 9 half-pint jars
Ingredients:

    1 lb. Velveeta cheese
    5 oz. canned evaporated milk
    ½ teaspoon salt
    1 tablespoon vinegar
    ½ teaspoon dry mustard

NOTE:

This cheese recipe is not approved by the National Center for food preservation, "rebel"Canners have been known to can cheese. It's just not tested and approved.It's not a beginner canning project

Nutrition:189 kCal

Mangolicious Butter

Preparation Time: 10 minutes
Cooking Time: 1 hour
Servings:6 pint jars
Ingredients:

    6 ½ cups ripe mangoes (peeled, pitted, chopped)
    3 tablespoon lemon juice
    2 ½ cups sugar
    ¾ cup orange juice
    ½ cup water

Directions:

Sterilize the jars. Combine the orange juice, mangoes and water in a pot and bring to boil. Simmer for 35 minutes on a reduced flame. Push the mixture through a wire sieve and then return the mushy mango back to the pan, mixing in the sugar and lemon juice.
Stir the mix until the sugar dissolves and then cook for another 30 minutes.
Skim off the foam.
Ladle the mix immediately into the sterilized jars, up to three-fourths full.
Get rid of any air bubbles and clean the rims.
Cover the jars with the lid and apply the bands making sure that it is tightened.
Submerge the jars within a prepared boiling water canner for 10 minutes.
Remove, allow to cool, and then label the jars.
Nutrition: 66 kCal

Raisin Plum Conserves

Preparation Time: 10 minutes
Cooking Time: 45 minutes
Servings: 7 half-pint jars
Ingredients:

- 5 cups plums (chopped, pitted)
- 1 cup orange (peeled, seeded, chopped)
- 3 cups sugar
- 1 cup raisins
- 1 cup pecans (chopped)
- 2 tablespoon orange rind
- 1 teaspoon cinnamon

Directions:

Sterilize the jars.

Mix together all the mentioned ingredients in a pot apart from the pecans and bring to boil.

Stir until you deserve the sugar and then cook until the gelling point, for around 15 minutes, stirring constantly.

Mix in the pecans and stir cook for another 5 minutes.

Turn-off the flame and skim-off any visible foam.

Ladle the mix immediately into the sterilized jars, leaving a quarter-inch of headspace.

Get rid of any air bubbles and clean the rims.

Cover the jars with the lid and apply the bands making sure that it is tightened.

Submerge the jars within a prepared boiling water canner for 15 minutes.

Remove, allow to cool, and then label the jars.

Nutrition: 95 kCal

Cinnamon Flavored Peach Butter

Preparation Time: 15 minutes

Cooking Time: 1 hour

Servings: 3 pint jars

    4 lbs. peaches (pitted, quartered)

    ¼ cup lemon juice

    2 cups sugar

    2 cups water

    2 tablespoon lemon zest (grated)

    2 teaspoon cinnamon

Directions:

Sterilize the jars.

Combine the water and peaches in a pan and bring to boil.

Simmer until tender, stirring frequently.

Process the mixture in batches till smooth.

Transfer the mixture into the pan again and mix in the lemon juice, lemon zest, sugar, and cinnamon.

Bring to boil again, stirring constantly.

Simmer for around 30 minutes, stirring often.

Turn-off the flame and skim-off any visible foam.

Ladle the mix immediately into the sterilized jars, leaving a quarter-inch of headspace.

Get rid of any air bubbles and clean the rims.

Cover the jars with the lid and apply the bands making sure that it is tightened.

Submerge the jars within a prepared boiling water canner for 10 minutes.

Remove, allow to cool, and then label the jars.

Nutrition: 59 kCal

Spiced Pear Butter

Preparation Time: 25 minutes
Cooking Time: 1 hour and 30 minutes
Servings: 9 half-pint jars
Ingredients:

- 15 Bartlett pears (sliced)
- 1 teaspoon cloves (ground)
- 1 ½ teaspoon cinnamon (ground)
- 2 cups water
- 2 tablespoon lemon juice
- 6 cups sugar
- ½ teaspoon ginger (ground)

Directions:

Sterilize the jars.

Combine water and pears in a pan and cook covered until tender (approx. 30 minutes)

Press the tender pears in a colander and then measure 8 cups of pear pulp.

Transfer the pear pulp back into the pan.

In a separate pan caramelize 1 ½ cups of water, stirring and then transfer it into the pear pulp.

Mix in the left over ingredients except for the lemon juice and cook for around 45 minutes uncovered till thickened, stirring frequently.

Turn-off the flame and skim-off any visible foam.

Ladle the mix immediately into the sterilized jars, leaving a quarter-inch of headspace.

Get rid of any air bubbles and clean the rims.

Cover the jars with the lid and apply the bands making sure that it is tightened.

Submerge the jars within a prepared boiling water canner for 15 minutes.

Remove, allow to cool, and then label the jars.

Nutrition: 88 kCal

Pear & Cherry Conserves

Preparation Time: 25 minutes
Cooking Time: 1 hour
Servings: 10 pint jars
Ingredients:

- 8 cups ripe pears (chopped)
- 32 oz. tart cherries (canned, drained)
- 32 oz. pineapple (canned, undrained)
- 2 limes (zest grated)
- 2 lemons (zest grated)
- 2 cups raisins
- 10 cups sugar
- 1 1/3 cups walnuts (chopped coarsely)

Directions:

Sterilize the jars.

Combine the lime and lemon zest and fruit, pineapple, cherries, pears, sugar and raisins in bowl and leave to refrigerate overnight.

Place the mixture into a Dutch oven and cook for 50-60 minutes till it thickens.

Mix in the nuts.

Turn-off the flame and skim-off any visible foam.

Ladle the mix immediately into the sterilized jars, leaving a quarter-inch of headspace.

Get rid of any air bubbles and clean the rims.

Cover the jars with the lid and apply the bands making sure that it is tightened.

Submerge the jars within a prepared boiling water canner for 10 minutes.

Remove, allow to cool, and then label the jars.

Nutrition: 70 kCal

CHAPTER 9:

Pressure Canning: Meat

Canned Beef Stroganoff

Preparation Time: 30 minutes
Cooking Time: 75 minutes
Servings: 6
Ingredients:
1-teaspoon black pepper
2 teaspoons salt
2 teaspoons thyme
2 teaspoons parsley
4 tablespoons Worcestershire sauce
2 cloves of garlic, minced
1 cup mushrooms, sliced
1 cup onion, chopped
2 pounds stewing beef, cut into chunks
4 cups beef broth
Directions:
Sterilize the bottles in a pressure canner as indicated in the general guidelines. Allow the bottles to cool.

Place all the needed ingredients in a pot and boil for 10 minutes. Reduce the heat and allow simmering for another 30 minutes. Turn off the heat and allow cooling slightly. Transfer mixture to sterilized bottles.

Remove air bubbles and close jars.

Place the jars in a pressure canner and process for 75 minutes.

Nutrition:207 kCal

Canned Ground Beef

Preparation Time: 15 minutes
Cooking Time: 75 minutes
Servings: 5
Ingredients:
2 pounds ground beef
3 cups water
Pickling salt
Directions:
Sterilize the bottles in a pressure canner as indicated in the general guidelines. Allow the bottles to cool.

Place beef in a skillet and sauté the meat for 10 minutes until browned.

Pack the meat loosely in the sterilized bottles. Set aside.

Using a pan, bring water to a boil and add ½-teaspoon canning salt per pint of water. Stir to dissolve the salt.

Pour the canning liquid over the beef and leave 1-inch headspace.

Remove air bubbles and close jars.

Place the jars in a pressure canner and process for 75 minutes.

Nutrition:392 kCal

Canned Chipotle Beef

Preparation Time: 15 minutes
Cooking Time: 75 minutes
Servings: 6
Ingredients:
2 pounds beef brisket, cut into chunks
2 teaspoons salt
8 cloves of garlic, minced
2 cups onion, chopped
2 teaspoons oregano
½-cup coriander
2 chipotle chilies, chipped
4 cups beef broth
Directions:
Sterilize the bottles in a pressure canner as indicated in the general guidelines. Allow the bottles to cool.
Place the beef in a pot and also season it with salt. Turn on the heat and sear all sides for 3 minutes. Stir in the garlic and onion. Cook for another minute. Add in the rest of the ingredients.
Close the lid, allowing the meat to simmer for 20 minutes on medium heat. Turn off the heat and allow the mixture to slightly cool.
Transfer the mixture to the bottles.
Remove air bubbles and close jars.
Place the jars in a pressure canner and process for 75 minutes.
Nutrition:322 kCal

Canned Pork

Preparation Time: 15 minutes
Cooking Time: 75 minutes
Servings: 5
Ingredients:

      2 pounds pork chops, boneless
      Canning salt
      Water

Directions:

Sterilize the bottles in a pressure canner as indicated in the general guidelines. Allow the bottles to cool.

Place the pork chops in boiling water and allow simmering for 15 minutes. Strain the cooked pork and pack them in the sterilized bottles.

Using a pan, bring water to a boil and add ½-teaspoon canning salt per pint of water. Stir to dissolve the salt.

Pour pickling solution into the bottle to cover the pork. Leave an inch of headspace.

Remove air bubbles and close jars.

Place the jars in a pressure canner and process for 75 minutes. Follow the guidelines for pressure canning.

Nutrition: 379 kCal

Canned Chili

Preparation Time: 15 minutes
Cooking time: 75 minutes
Servings: 6
Ingredients:

3 cups of dry kidney beans, soaked overnight and drained
2 pounds ground beef
1 cup onion, chopped
1 cup pepper, seeded and chopped
4 cups tomatoes, chopped
1 tablespoon chili pepper, seeded and chopped

Directions:

Sterilize the bottles in a pressure canner as indicated in the general guidelines. Allow the bottles to cool.   Place the beans in a pot and boil for 30 minutes. Drain the beans.

To a clean pot, put the cooked beans and the rest of the ingredients. Cook for another 20 minutes. Transfer the mixture into the sterilized bottles. Leave an inch of headspace.

Remove air bubbles and close jars.

Place the jars in a pressure canner and process for 75 minutes. Follow the guidelines for pressure canning.

Nutrition: 412 kCal

Ground/Chopped Beef, Pork, Lamb, or Sausage

Preparation Time: 10 min
Cooking Time: 1 hour
Servings: 2
Ingredients:
Preferred meat, fresh, chilled, chopped/ground
Salt (1 teaspoon for each quart jar)
Meat broth, boiling/tomato juice/water
Directions:
Chop the chilled fresh meat into small chunks. If using venison, grind after mixing with one cup of pork fat (high quality) to every three to four cups of venison. If using sausage (freshly made), combine with cayenne pepper and salt.
Shape into meatballs or patties. If using cased sausage, chop into three to four -inch links.
Cook the meat until light brown in color. If using ground meat, sauté without shaping.
Add the cooked meat to clean and hot Mason jars. Each filled with salt (1 teaspoon).
Boil the meat broth. Pour the meat broth, tomato juice, or water into the jars until filled up to one inch from the top.
Remove air bubbles before adjusting the lids, then process in the pressure canner for 1 hour and 15 minutes (pints) or 1 hour and 30 minutes (quarts).
Nutrition:642 kCal

Beef Stew

Preparation Time: 10 min
Cooking Time: 75 min
Servings: 4
Ingredients:
3 tbsp. flour
2 pounds canned beef
1 package beef stew seasoning mix powder
2 tbsp. vegetable oil
5 cups frozen bagged vegetables
3 cups water
Directions:
Toss beef in flour, then browns in oil in a skillet over medium-high heat.
Stir in water and seasoning.
Add frozen vegetables and bring to a boil.
Turn to low.
Cover and simmer for 75 minutes.
Nutrition:768kCal

Meat Stock

Preparation Time: 10 min
Cooking Time: +1 hour
Servings: 2
Ingredients:
Beef/chicken bones
Water
Directions:
If making beef broth:

After cracking the beef bones (fresh trimmed), rinse and place in a stockpot filled with enough water to cover the bones. Heat until boiling. Afterwards, simmer for about three to four hours.

Discard the bones and let the broth cool before skimming excess fat. Reheat the broth and then pour into clean and hot Mason jars, each with a one-inch headspace remaining.

Adjust the lids after removing air bubbles and process in the pressure canner for 20 minutes (pints) or 25 minutes (quarts).

If making chicken/turkey broth:

Fill a large stockpot with your large chicken or turkey bones. Pour some water into it, enough to cover the bones, then cover and simmer for thirty to forty-five minutes.

Discard the bones and let the broth cool before removing excess fat. Reheat before pouring into clean and hot Mason jars, each left with one-inch headspace.

Adjust the jar lids before processing in the pressure canner for 75 minutes (for pint jars) or 90 minutes (for quart jars).

Nutrition:361 kCal

Chile Con Carne
Preparation Time: 10 min
Cooking Time: 1 hour
Servings: 2
Ingredients:
Water (5 ½ cups)
Tomatoes, whole/crushed (2 quarts)
Peppers, chopped (1 cup)
Beef, ground (3 pounds)
Chili powder (5 tablespoons)
Red kidney/pinto beans, dried (3 cups)
Salt divided (5 teaspoons)
Onions, chopped (1 ½ cups)
Black pepper (1 teaspoon)
Directions:
Thoroughly wash the beans before adding them to a saucepan (2-quart). Cover with cold water and let sit for twelve hours.
Drain the beans that have been soaked and place in a saucepan filled with freshwater (5 ½ cups) and salt (2 teaspoons). Stir to combine and heat until boiling, then simmer for half an hour.
Drain the cooked beans and then return to the saucepan. Stir in salt (3 teaspoons), chili powder, pepper, and tomatoes. Simmer the mixture for five minutes; avoid letting the mixture thicken.
Pour the mixture into clean and hot Mason jars, each with a one-inch headspace remaining. Get rid of any air bubbles before adjusting the jar lids.
Put in the pressure canner and process for 1 hour and 25 minutes.
Nutrition: 464 kCal

Beef Paprika

Preparation Time: 10 min
Cooking Time: 1 hour
Servings: 6
Ingredients:
1 sliced onion
2 tbsp. flour
1/4 tsp. black pepper
1/4 tsp. salt
2 minced cloves of garlic
2 chopped red bell peppers
2 tbsp. sweet paprika
1/2 cup beef broth
2 tbsp. tomato paste
1/2 cup sour cream
1 tsp. caraway seeds
1/4 cup chopped fresh dill
2 pounds canned beef
Directions:
Place onions in a slow cooker.
In a small bowl, toss the beef in flour with salt and pepper.
Top onions with seasoned beef.
Spread over garlic and bell peppers in the slow cooker.
In a separate small bowl, combine paprika, broth, caraway, and tomato paste.
Pour sauce over beef.
Cover to cook, put on high for 4 hours or low for 8 hours.
Uncover and turn off heat; let stand for 10 minutes.
Stir in dill and sour cream.
Nutrition:768 kCal

Grilled Venison

Preparation Time: 10 min
Cooking Time: 1 hour
Servings: 4
Ingredients:
2 pounds canned venison
1 -1/2 pounds sliced bacon
1-quart apple cider
24 oz. bottled barbecue sauce or marinade
Directions:
Place venison on a shallow baking dish and cover in apple cider.
Cover with plastic wrap and refrigerate for 2 hours.
Remove and pat the meat dry, then discard apple cider and place venison back in the baking dish. Pour barbecue sauce over venison, cover again, and refrigerate for 2 hours more.
Preheat an outdoor grill to high heat.
Remove the meat from the refrigerator then let it stand for 30 minutes.
Wrap pieces of venison in bacon.
Place bacon-wrapped venison pieces onto grill grate, not touching each other.
Grill for 20 minutes, constantly turning it.
Nutrition:690 kCal

Italian Beef

Preparation Time: 10 min
Cooking Time: 1 hour
Servings: 4
Ingredients:
4 toasted baguettes
16oz beef broth
1 pound canned beef
Toppings of your choice (peppers, onions, cheese, etc.)
Directions:
Brown beef for 5 minutes per side in the skillet, over medium-high heat.
Add broth and bring to a boil.
After this, turn heat to medium-low and immediately simmer until slightly reduced.
Spoon onto baguettes.
Top with toppings of your choice.
Nutrition:690 kCal

Apricot Pork

Preparation Time: 10 min
Cooking Time: 1 hour
Servings: 4
Ingredients:
1/2 tsp. salt
1/2 tsp. dried thyme
1 pound canned pork
2 tbsp. olive oil
1 sliced onion
1 tbsp. butter
2 tbsp. apricot jam
1/2 cup chicken broth
1 tbsp. Dijon mustard
Directions:
Sprinkle pork with salt and thyme on both sides.
Cook in oil over medium-high heat in a skillet for 3 minutes per side; do not crowd.
Remove from skillet, and then melt butter in skillet.
Cook onion for 3 minutes. After which, add jam, mustard, and broth.
Bring to a boil, stirring continuously.
Cover and turn heat to medium-low, then simmer for 5 minutes.
Return pork to skillet and stir to coat in sauce.
Again, cover and simmer for at least 5 minutes more to heat pork through.
Nutrition: 768 kCal

CHAPTER 10:

Pressure Canning Recipes: Other Options

Rhubarb Jam
Preparation Time: 25 minutes
Cooking Time: 45 minutes
Servings: 32
Ingredients:

> 2 1/2 pounds fresh rhubarb, chopped 2
> cups white sugar
> 2 teaspoons grated orange zest
> 1/3 cup orange juice
> 1/2 cup water

Directions:
Boil water, orange juice, orange zest, sugar and rhubarb in a saucepan; cook for 45 minutes on medium low heat till thick, occasionally mixing; as it cools, it thickens more.
Put in hot sterile jars; seal with rings and lids. Keep opened jars in the fridge.
Nutrition: 57 kCal

Rhubarb Compote with Ginger

Preparation Time: 10 minutes
Cooking Time: 15 minutes
Servings: 4
Ingredients:

> 1 pound chopped rhubarb
> 1/2 cup orange juice
> 1 1/2 cups sugar, or more
> 2 tablespoons chopped candied ginger

Directions:

In a large glass or ceramic jar, mix together candied ginger, orange juice, sugar and rhubarb. Let it stand overnight or for a minimum of 8 hours. Pour the rhubarb mixture into a pot to boil for about 15 minutes over medium-low heat. Use sugar to sweeten and transfer it to a clean jar. Use the lid to cover well and put it into the refrigerator to store up to 1 week.
Nutrition: 338 kCal

Kale Slaw

Preparation Time: 30 minutes
Cooking Time: 1 week
Servings: 4
Ingredients:

> 3 cups kale leaves
> 2 carrots
> 1 cup small broccoli florets
> ½ medium onion
> Starter culture (optional)
> 1 tablespoon unrefined sea salt
> Filtered water

Directions:

Wash the vegetables. Cleave or shred the kale leaves. Shred the carrots. Cut the broccoli florets into little pieces. Dice the onion. Put the entirety of the vegetables in a glass bowl and combine them. Create brine by mixing the sea salt with 4 cups of sifted water and mixing the salt in until it dissolves. Include the starter culture now in case you're going to utilize it. Put the vegetables in the fermenting compartment. Pack them in firmly. Empty brine into the compartment until it's directly over the top of the vegetables. Place a load in the container and also press it down to squeeze any air pockets out of the vegetables. The brine ought to be over the top of load when you're finished squeezing it down. Ensure you leave several inches of headspace at the head of the container in light of the fact that the salt in the saline solution will haul more moisture out of the vegetables. Place the cover or lid on the container and let it age at room temperature for as long as seven days. Check it the following week and move it to the ice chest in case you're content with the aging. If not, let it ferment until you feel it's prepared.
Nutrition: 57 kCal

Rhubarb and Blueberry Compote
Preparation Time: 40 minutes
Cooking Time: 30 minutes
Servings: 8
Ingredients:
- 10 stalks rhubarb, peeled and chopped
- 1 cup white sugar
- 1 cup frozen blueberries
- 1 teaspoon vanilla extract
- 1 cinnamon stick
- water to cover

Directions:
Mix cinnamon stick, vanilla extract, blueberries, sugar and rhubarb in a pot. To barely cover rhubarb, add sufficient water. Simmer for 30-40 minutes till rhubarb is broken down and soft, occasionally mixing. Dispose of cinnamon stick.
Cool compote for 30 minutes till thick in the fridge.
Nutrition: 112 kCal

Rhubarb Pineapple Jam
Preparation Time: 10 minutes
Cooking Time: 20 minutes
Servings: 7
Ingredients:
- 10 cups chopped fresh rhubarb
- 1 (20 ounces) can crush pineapple, undrained 2
- cups white sugar
- 1 (6ounces) package strawberry flavored Jell-Q®

Directions:
Boil sugar, pineapple and rhubarb in a big saucepan on medium heat; mix and cook for 20 minutes till rhubarb is tender. Take off from the heat; mix in gelatin till fully blended. Put into plastic containers/glass jars; freeze/refrigerate.
Nutrition: 49 kCal

CHAPTER 11:

Fermenting Recipes: Relish

Dill Relish

Preparation Time: 3 hours
Cooking Time: 40 minutes
Servings: 64
Ingredients:
  6 cups cucumbers, chopped
  2 cups sweet red peppers, chopped
  1 cup celery, chopped
  2/3 cup pickling salt
  6 cups cold water
  4 cups white vinegar
  1 cup sugar
  2 Tbsp. mustard seed
  ½ cup fresh dill heads, chopped
Directions:
Remove seeds and ribs of peppers, then stems and blossom ends of cucumbers. Chop vegetables with a coarse blade on a meat grinder.

Combine cucumber, pepper, onion, and celery with salt and water. Let sit for 3 hours. Drain, rinse thoroughly using cold water, and drain well once more. Bring vinegar, sugar, and remaining fixings to a bubble in an enormous pot, stirring to dissolve sugar. Include drained, chopped vegetables and return to a boil. Minimize to simmer and continue until relish reaches desired consistency—about 15 minutes.

Ladle hot relish into half-pint jars, leaving ½ inch of headspace. Wipe rim of jar clean; place hot, simmered beforehand lid on the jar, and screw down ring firmly tight. Set in a boiling water bath canner for 25 minutes.

Nutrition: 6 kCal

Beet Relish

Preparation Time: 15 minutes
Cooking Time: 20 minutes
Servings: 4 pints
Ingredients:

  1 quart chopped, cooked beets
  1-quart chopped cabbage
  1 cup chopped onion
  1 cup chopped sweet red pepper
  1½ cup sugar
  1 Tbsp. prepared horseradish
  1 Tbsp. pickling salt
  3 cups white vinegar

Directions:

Combine all ingredients in a large pot. Slowly simmer for 10 minutes. Bring to a boil, then quickly pack hot into hot jars, leaving ¼ inch of headspace. Wipe rim of jar clean; place hot, simmered beforehand lid on the jar, and screw down ring firmly tight. Set it up for 15 minutes in a boiling water bath canner.

Nutrition: 34 kCal

Chow-chow Relish

Preparation Time: 15 minutes
Cooking Time: 40 minutes
Servings: 4 pints
Ingredients:

- 1 medium head cabbage, chopped
- 6 medium onions
- 6 sweet green peppers
- 6 sweet red peppers
- 1-quart hard green tomatoes
- ¼ cup pickling salt
- 2 Tbsp. prepared mustard
- 1½ quarts white vinegar
- 2½ cups sugar
- 1½ tsp. ground ginger
- 2 Tbsp. mustard seed
- 1 Tbsp. celery seed
- 1 Tbsp. mixed whole pickling spice

Directions:

Rinse vegetables. Remove seeds and ribs from peppers. Chop all vegetables in a meat grinder with a coarse blade. Mix with salt. Cover. Let it stand in a cool place overnight. Drain.

In a large pot, mix mustard with a small amount of vinegar; add remaining vinegar, sugar, and spices. Boil it, and then simmer for 30 minutes. Add vegetables. Simmer 10 minutes. Quickly pack hot relish into hot, sterilized jars, leaving ¼ inch of headspace. Be sure liquid covers vegetables. Wipe rim of jar clean; place hot, simmered beforehand lid on the jar, and screw down ring firmly tight. Set it up for 10 minutes in a boiling water bath canner.

Nutrition: 15 kCal

Corn Relish

Preparation Time: 15 minutes
Cooking Time: 30 minutes
Servings: 4 pints
Ingredients:

  9 cups fresh sweet corn
  2 cups chopped onions
  1 cup chopped green peppers
  ½ cup chopped red peppers
  1 cup sugar
  2 Tbsp. salt
  1½ Tbsp. celery seed
  1½ Tbsp. mustard seed
  1 Tbsp. turmeric
  3 cups cider vinegar

Directions:
Cut corn from ears. Remove stems, seeds, and ribs from peppers. Combine chopped vegetables, sugar, salt, spices, and vinegar. Bring to a boil. Cover and simmer 15 minutes, stirring once in a while to prevent scorching. Scoop hot relish into hot, sterilized jars, leaving ¼ inch of headspace. Wipe rim of jar clean; place hot, simmered beforehand lid on the jar, and screw down ring firmly tight. Set in a boiling water bath canner for 15 minutes.
Nutrition:21 kCal

Pepper Relish

Preparation Time: 15 minutes
Cooking Time: 20 minutes
Servings: 4 pints
Ingredients:

  12 sweet red peppers
  12 sweet green peppers
  12 medium onions
  2 cups white vinegar
  2 cups sugar
  3 Tbsp. pickling salt

Directions:
Remove ribs and seeds from peppers. Chop vegetables with a meat grinder, using a coarse blade. Cover with boiling water. Let stand 5 minutes, then drain. Add the rest of the other ingredients and bring to a boil. Simmer 5 minutes. Scoop hot relish into hot, sterilized jars, leaving ¼ inch of headspace. Wipe rim of jar clean; place hot, simmered beforehand lid on the jar, and screw down ring firmly tight. Set in a 15-minute boiling water bath canner.
Nutrition:10 kCal

Piccalilli

Preparation Time: 15 minutes
Cooking Time: 40 minutes
Servings: 4 pints
Ingredients:

- 2 quarts green tomatoes
- ½ cup pickling salt
- 1-pint white vinegar
- ¼ cup mustard seed
- 1 tsp. cinnamon
- 1 tsp. dry mustard
- 1 tsp. allspice
- 1 tsp. ground cloves
- 1 tsp. celery seed
- ½ tsp. pepper
- 2 green peppers
- 2 chopped onions
- 3 cups sugar

Directions:

Chop tomatoes in the meat grinder, using a coarse knife. Sprinkle with a salt, press down, and let stand, covered, overnight in a cool place. Then drain well.

Combine vinegar and spices in a large pot and bring to a boil. Seed and chop peppers and onion. Add vegetables and sugar to the kettle and bring to a boil. Simmer for 30 minutes, stirring as needed. Pack hot relish into hot, cleaned containers, leaving ¼ inch of headspace. Wipe the edge of the container clean; place the hot sterilized lid on the jar, and screw down ring firmly tight. Set in a boiling water bath canner for 10 minutes.

Nutrition: 16 kCal

Apple Relish
Preparation Time: 15 minutes
Cooking Time: 20 minutes
Servings: 4 pints
Ingredients:

>4 lbs. apples
>3 quarts water
>1¼ cups white vinegar, divided
>1 cup sugar
>½ cup light corn syrup
>2/3 cup water
>2 tsp. whole cloves
>1½ sticks cinnamon

Directions:

Wash, pare, core, and also cut apples into eighths. Place in a bowl containing 3 quarts water and 4 Tbsp. vinegar to prevent darkening.

Combine sugar, corn syrup, rest of vinegar, 2/3 cup water, cloves, and cinnamon, broken into pieces, in a pot. Heat to boiling. Drain apples and add to the pot. Cover and boil for 3 minutes, stirring occasionally. Scoop hot relish into hot, sterilized jars, leaving ¼ inch of headspace, filling with syrup, leaving ¼ inch of headspace. Wipe rim of jar clean; place hot, simmered beforehand lid on the jar, and screw down rim firmly tight. Set in a10-minute boiling water bath canner.Tip: This relish is good served with pork or poultry.

Nutrition:53.1 kCal

Elderberry Relish

Preparation Time: 15 minutes
Cooking Time: 20 minutes
Servings: 4 pints
Ingredients:

  3 pints ripe elderberries
  1½ pints white vinegar
  1½ cups sugar
  1 Tbsp. cinnamon
  1 Tbsp. allspice
  1 Tbsp. cloves
  ¼ tsp. cayenne pepper

Directions:

Stem elderberries and rinse. Add to vinegar and gently simmer to soften elderberries. Press berries through a sieve. Return to vinegar. Add sugar and spices and simmer until it begins to thicken. Stir frequently to prevent scorching. Scoop hot relish into hot, sterilized jars, leaving ¼ inch of headspace. Set in a10-minutes boiling water bath canner.
Nutrition:50 kCal

Aunt Katie's relish

Preparation Time: 15 minutes
Cooking Time: 15 minutes
Servings: 4 pints
Ingredients:

  24 ripe medium tomatoes
  8 peaches
  8 pears
  8 apples
  3 onions
  2 cups cider vinegar
  4 cups sugar
  2 Tbsp. salt
  2 Tbsp. mixed pickling spices

Directions:

Peel, core, seed, and chop tomatoes, peaches, pears, apples, and onions. Dissolve the mixture of sugar and salt in vinegar in a large pot. Mix in all ingredients, with spices in spice bag. Boil and then and simmer until relish is thick, stirring frequently to avoid scorching. Scoop hot relish into hot, sterilized jars, leaving ¼ inch of headspace. Wipe rim of jar clean; place hot, simmered beforehand lid on the jar, and screw down ring firmly tight. Set in a10-minutes boiling water bath canner. **Nutrition:**32 kCal

Rhubarb Relish
Preparation Time: 15 minutes
Cooking Time: 15 minutes
Servings: 4 pints
Ingredients:
> 2 quarts rhubarb
> 1-quart white onions, peeled and sliced
> 4 cups brown sugar
> 1 cup cider vinegar
> 2 tsp. salt

Spice bag:
> 1 Tbsp. cinnamon
> 1 Tbsp. ginger
> 1 Tbsp. mixed pickling spices

Directions:
Cut rhubarb into ½ inch pieces. Do not use leaves; they are poisonous. Do not skin stalks. Mix all the mentioned ingredients and slowly bring to a boil. Simmer until rhubarb is tender but not mushy. Remove spice bag. Scoop hot relish into hot, sterilized jars, leaving ¼ inch of headspace. Wipe rim of jar clean; place hot, simmered beforehand lid on the jar, and screw down ring firmly tight. Set it up for 10 minutes in a boiling water bath canner.
Nutrition:11 kCal

CHAPTER 12:

Fermenting Recipes: Wine

Red Rowan Wine
Preparation Time: 30 minutes
Cooking Time: 3 months
Servings: 1
Ingredients:
    2 kg rowanberries
    5 lbs. sugar
    1 tsp. yeast nutrient
    4L water ·
Directions:
Crush the berries, add 2 pounds of sugar, yeast, and water. After a week, add 2 more pounds of sugar, stir, and let it sit for another week. Add the remaining sugar, stir, insert an airlock or fix a rubber glove with one-two holes made with a needle. Let it ferment for three months. You'll know the wine is ready in the absence of bubbles.

You may use plastic wrap instead of a rubber glove (you need to fix the plastic wrap with a rubber band). Carbon dioxide emitted during the fermentation process will stretch the rubber band and get out, but oxygen won't be able to get in.

Nutrition: 172 kCal

Rhubarb Wine

Preparation Time: 1 hour
Cooking Time: 2 weeks
Servings: 1
Ingredients:

>   3.5 lbs. rhubarb
>   1 tsp. yeast
>   4 lbs. sugar

Directions:

Press juice from the rhubarb, dilute it with water in a 1:1 ratio, and add 4 pounds of sugar for each every 2 quarts of the solution. Bottle, add a handful of unwashed raisins, cover with a cheesecloth, and let it sit in a warm place for 3 days.

Cover using plastic wrap and fix it with a rubber band. Store in a warm place at a temperature not lower than 75-77°.

After the wine ferments, use a rubber tube to transfer the wine into a different container. Remove sediment and foam, thoroughly wash the bottle, and transfer the wine back into it. Add 2 pounds of sugar, cover the bottle with plastic wrap, and repeat this process after 10 days. Bottle the wine after it ferments and lightens and stores it in a cool place.

Nutrition: 249 kCal

Cherry Brandy

Preparation Time: 10 minutes
Cooking Time: 2-3 months
Servings: 1
Ingredients:

Washed ripe berries
35 mL Vodka
Water (optional)
Sugar (optional)

Directions:
Fill 1/3 of the bottle with washed ripe berries and then pour vodka into it until it fills up completely. Plug the bottle with a cotton ball and leave it in a sunny spot for 2-3 months. Over the course of these months, shake the bottle 2 times a week. Strain the brandy and pour it into sterile bottles. If the brandy turns out too strong, you can dilute it with water in a 4:1 ratio and add ½ cup of sugar to each bottle. It'd be best to boil the water together with the sugar beforehand.
Nutrition: 132 kCal

Apple Vinegar with Honey

Preparation Time: 30 minutes
Cooking Time: 3 months
Servings: 1
Ingredients:

1 quart of apple puree
1 quart of water
1/2 cup of honey (or sugar)
1 teaspoon of yeast
1 piece of rye bread

Directions:
Wash and grind apples of any kind without peeling them.
Add boiled water and stir in half of the honey. Add yeast and bread. Make sure that no more than 2/3 of the volume of the dish that you're using is filled. Let the vinegar ferment for 10 days. Stir it daily.
Filter the vinegar through a folded cheesecloth. Add the remaining honey and let it sit for 2 more months.
Filter through cotton wool and bottle. The vinegar can be stored at room temperature.
Nutrition: 130 kCal

Cranberry Liquor
Preparation Time: 15 minutes
Cooking Time: 20 minutes or 3 weeks
Servings: 1
Ingredients:
For the first method:
   1 quart of vodka
   1 cup of sugar
   1 cup of cranberry juice
For the second method:
   2 ¼ cup of cranberries
   1 ⅓ cups of sugar
   1 quart of quality vodka
Directions:
First method
Dissolve sugar in cranberry juice and cook over medium heat without bringing it to a boil. As soon as the sugar dissolves, remove it from heat, chill, and add vodka.
Stir and bottle. The drink can be served right away.
Second method
Crush the berries and mix them with sugar. Add vodka and let it sit for at least 3 weeks. Then filter, let the liquor settle, and serve.
Nutrition: 103 kCal

Dandelion "Whiskey"

Preparation Time: 45 minutes
Cooking Time: 7 months, 4 hours cooking
Servings: 1
Ingredients:

 4 cups of dandelion flowers
 1 quart of water
 2 ½ pounds of sugar
 Juice and zest of an orange & a lemon
 Pinch of ginger
 1 ounce of yeast
 a piece of rye bread

Directions:

Remove the petals from the flowers and put them in a bowl. Add boiling water and soak the petals for 3 days.

Transfer the contents of the bowl to a pot, add lemon and orange juices and zest, sugar, and ginger. Boil for half an hour, chill to human body temperature.

Rub yeast on the bread, put it into the pot, and cover.

When the rising foam goes down, strain, and bottle. Cork and leave it to ripen. If you prepare the "whiskey" in May it will be ready for Christmas.

Note: You can leave the bottle uncorked and add 3 chopped raisins and a pinch of sugar every month. This will make the wine stronger and it will start resembling whiskey.

Nutrition: 108 kCal

Cherry Liquor

Preparation Time: 1 hour
Cooking Time: 1-2 weeks
Servings: 1
Ingredients:

2 pounds of cherries
1 pound of sugar
1 quart of 70% alcohol

Directions:

Pit the cherries, crush them, and put them into a jar with a wide mouth. Add 70% alcohol or vodka (40% solution alcohol) and let it sit for a week. Don't use 96% alcohol because it will preserve the cherries. Shake twice a day.

Make sugar syrup using 2 cups of water (if you used vodka you need to add additional 2 cups of water), chill, and add it to the mixture. Let it sit for another week. Shake daily.

Filter the liquor through a napkin. It turns out delicious and beautiful. You can also make liquor from strawberries, raspberries, and other berries.

Nutrition: 157 kCal

Sherry Brandy Liquor

Preparation Time: 10 minutes
Cooking Time: 15 minutes
Servings: 1
Ingredients:

100 cherry leaves
1 cup of chokeberry (aronia)
4 cups of water

Directions:

Add chokeberries and cherry leaves to a pot of water, bring it to a boil, and cook for 10 minutes.

Remove from heat, chill, and strain (without pressing juice from the pulp).

Stir in 1 2/3 pounds of sugar and a teaspoon of citric acid and cook for 2-3 more minutes.

Chill and slowly stir in an alcohol solution (1 cup of alcohol to 1 cup of water). If you're using vodka instead of alcohol don't add water and instead just use 2 cups of vodka.

Nutrition: 195 kCal

Cream Liqueur "Raspberry King"
Preparation Time: 15 minutes
Cooking Time: 0 minutes
Servings: 1
Ingredients:
- 4 eggs
- 2 cups of raspberry jam
- 1 cup of cream
- 1 2/3 cups of vodka
- a small bag of vanilla sugar
- 2 tablespoons of cocoa
- 2 tablespoons of sugar

Directions:
Separate the egg yolks then beat them with sugar.
Mix cocoa with cream and stir well. Strain the raspberry jam.
Continuing to beat the yolks, gradually stir in cream, jam, and vodka.
Add vanilla sugar to the last.
Strain through a sieve and bottle. Serve the liquor shortly after.
Note: if you're using raspberry juice instead of jam, increase the sugar amount to 1/2 cup and use 1 cup of juice. Boil the juice with sugar beforehand (leaving 2 tablespoons for whipping the yolk). After you strain the jam, add cold water to the remains, stir, and strain through a sieve. You'll get a tasty drink!
Nutrition: 103 kCal

Aronia Liquor
Preparation Time: 10 minutes
Cooking Time: 20 minutes
Servings: 1
Ingredients:
- 3 pounds of berries
- 2 pounds of sugar
- 1 2/3 cups of water
- 1/2 teaspoon of citric acid
- 2 cups of vodka

Directions:
Boil berries and sugar for 20 minutes.
Chill. Get the berries out using a colander and strain the syrup through a sieve.
Add citric acid and vodka to the chilled syrup. Bottle. Spread the remaining berries on a wooden board and dry them. They will turn into raisins. Store them in closed glass jars.
Nutrition: 55 kCal

Raspberry Liquor
Preparation Time: 20 minutes
Cooking Time: 3-4 weeks
Servings: 1
Ingredients:
- 2 cups of raspberries
- 1 quart of 70% alcohol

Directions:
Put 2 cups of fresh raspberries into a wide-mouth bottle and add 1 quart of 70% alcohol.
Wrap the mouth of the bottle with a cloth and keep it in a cool place for 3-4 weeks.
Dissolve 2 cups of sugar in 2 cups of water, boil, chill, and stir into the bottle with raspberries.
Stir, filter, and bottle. The quality of this liquor increases over time.
Nutrition: 103 kCal

Cream Liquor "Charlie"
Preparation Time: 30 minutes
Cooking Time: 0 minutes
Servings: 1
Ingredients:
- 4 eggs
- 2 tablespoons of sugar
- 2 cups of milk
- 2 tablespoons of cocoa
- 2 cups of raspberry syrup
- 1 cup of alcohol
- 2 small bags of vanilla sugar

Directions:
Separate 4 yolks and whip them with 2 tablespoons of sugar.
Boil 2 cups of milk and stir in 2 tablespoons of cocoa.
Chill and start whipping while gradually stirring in the yolks.
Continuing to whip, gradually stir in raspberry syrup, alcohol, and vanilla sugar.
Strain twice through a fine sieve and bottle.
Serve shortly after.
Nutrition: 103 kCal

"Cognac" 44

Preparation Time: 45 minutes
Cooking Time: 44 days
Servings: 1
Ingredients:

  3 oranges
  44 roasted coffee beans
  44 teaspoons of sugar
  2 ½ quarts of vodka

Directions:

Wash the oranges, dry them with a towel, cut a medium-sized hole on the tops (like a cap).

Put coffee beans into the holes, cover them with the orange peels, and fix the peels with toothpicks. Use 11 coffee beans for each orange.

Put the oranges into a jar and add 44 teaspoons of sugar.

Add the vodka and leave the jar in a dark place at room temperature for 44 days.

Drain the liquid into a glass dish, press the oranges through a cheesecloth, filter the juice, cover the dish, and let it sit for a week. Quality cognac aroma will appear.

Separate from the sediment and bottle. You may serve it right away, but the "cognac" will get better with aging.

Nutrition: 260 kCal

CHAPTER 13:

Fermenting Recipes: Pickles

Pickled Grapes
Preparation Time: 15 minutes
Cooking Time: 1 day and 40 minutes
Servings:10
Ingredients:
  1 pound seed less red grapes
  1 1/2 cups apple cider vinegar
  1 cupofwater
  1 cup of raw sugar
  ½ redonion, cut into slices
  2 teaspoons yellow mustard seeds
  1 teaspoon whole black
peppercorns

1 cinnamonstick
1 bay leaf
1-star anise pod
1 whole allspice

Directions:

Remove stems and discard any bad grapes. Place grapes in a quart-size mason jar and set aside.

Combine vinegar, water, sugar, redonion, mustard seeds, peppercorns, cinnamon stick, bay leaf, star anise pod, and all spice in a saucepan; bring to a boil.

Reduce heat to low and simmer until onion is softened, about 10 minutes. Remove saucepan from heat and cool for 15 minutes.

Carefully pour the cooled liquid over grapes and gently swirl the jar to incorporate spices. Cover the jar and refrigerate 1 day before eating.

Nutrition: 120 kCal

Pickled Garlicand Jalapeno Peppers

Preparation Time: 15 minutes
Cooking Time: 1 hour and 35 minutes
Servings: 20
Ingredients:

2 1/2 cups white vinegar
1/2 cup olive oil
2 carrots, chopped into bite-size pieces
16 fresh jalapeno peppers, chopped ..
1 head garlic, peeled, or more to taste.
2 tbsp whole blackpeppercorns
2 tbsp ground coriander
2 tbsp kosher salt
2 tablespoons whole mustard seeds

Directions:

Using a pot, combine and boil white vinegar and oliveoil. Add carrots; simmer for 10 minutes, until tender.

Stir in jalapenos, garlic, peppercorns, coriander, salt, mustardseeds, and thyme; simmer until jalapenos soften, 5 to 10 minutes.

Pour the jalapeno mixture into 2 jars, making sure thatthe jalapenos are fully submerged in the vinegar mixture. Coolfor about 1 hour; cover and refrigerate.

Nutrition: 66 kCal

Nothing' Sweet about These Spicy Refrigerator Pickles

Preparation Time: 15 minutes
Cooking Time: 1 day and 55 minutes
Servings: 12
Ingredients:

- 1 1/4 cups water
- 1 1/4 cups white vinegar
- 2 1/2 teaspoons picklings alt
- 1 teaspoon whole Tellicherry peppercorns
- 1 teaspoon yellow mustard seeds
- 1/4 teaspoon crushed red pepper flakes
- 1/2 teaspoon brown mustard seeds
- 1/2 teaspoon white sugar
- 6 pickling cucumbers
- 1/4 small whiteonion, sliced
- 8 sprigs fresh dill1 clovegarlic, slightly crushed

Directions:

Combineyellowand brown mustard seeds, sugar, water, vinegar, salt, peppercorns, and crushed redpepper flakes in a saucepan over medium heat.

Cook5-7 minutes, until sugar and salt have dissolved. Allow mixture to cool, about 30 minutes.

Cut cucumbers into even spears then pack into a 1-liter, large-mouthed glass jar.

Add onion slices, dill sprigs, and garlic. Pour cooled vinegar mixture over cucumbers in the jar to cover completely.

Seal and refrigerate for 24 hours before serving.

Nutrition: 26 kCal

QuickPickledRadishes

Preparation Time: 15 minutes
Cooking Time: 40 minutes
Servings: 4
Ingredients:

- 10 radishes, thinly sliced
- 2/3 cup white wine vinegar
- 1/3 cup water1 tablespoon white sugar
- 1 teaspoon salt
- 1star anise pod
- 1/2 teaspooncuminseed
- 1/2 teaspoon black peppercorns

Directions:

Place radish slicesinto a pint-sizedjar.

Heatwater and vinegar in a small non-reactive saucepan over medium heat; whisk in salt and sugar until just dissolved.

Remove from heat and add star anise pod, cumin seed, and black peppercorns.

Letcool slightly for 5 to 10 minutes.

Pour liquid over radishes. Cover andlet cool to room temperature, then refrigerate.

Nutrition: 17 kCal

Sour CherryPickle
Preparation Time: 5 minutes
Cooking Time: 21 days, 1 hour and 5 minutes
Servings: 8
Ingredients:
   1 cup sour cherries, not pitted
   1/2 teaspoon salt
   1 cup good quality white vinegar, or as need
Directions:
Wash then drain the cherries, place them on a metal baking sheet, and set them in the sun for 1 hour to be sure they are dry.
Place cherries in a jar with a plastic lid; add salt. Pour vinegar to fill the jar.
Close the lid and set aside for taste and color to ripen, 3 to 4 weeks. Refrigerate.
Nutrition: 29 kCal

Pickled Turnips
PreparationTime: 10 minutes
Cooking Time: 7 days and 17 minutes
Servings: 8
Ingredients:
   2 turnips, peeled and sliced into ½-inch wedges
   1 small beet, thinly sliced
   2 cloves garlic, chopped
   1 cup distilled white vinegar
   1 cup water
   1 teaspoon white sugar
   1 teaspoon sea salt
Directions:
Divide turnips, beet, and garlic between two 16-ounce masonjars.
Combine and boil vinegar, water, sugar, and salt in a saucepan for 2 minutes. Remove from heat and pour over turnips, leaving 1/2 inch of space on top. Seal jars and refrigerate for 1 week.
Nutrition: 16 kCal

Addictive Spicy Dill AvocadoPickles

PreparationTime: 10 minutes
Cooking Time:1 day and 30 minutes
Servings: 4
Ingredients:

  1 1/4 cups distilledwhitevinegar
  1 cupfiltered water1/2 cup whitesugar
  1 teaspoon rocksalt
  1 teaspoon brown mustard seeds
  1 teaspoon chopped fresh dill
  ½ teaspoon whole black peppercorns
  ½ teaspoon habanero pepper flakes
  2 habanero peppers
  1 clove garlic, lightly smashed and halved
  2 under ripe avocados, peeled and sliced into eighths.

Directions:

Using a saucepan, combine vinegar and water.

Stir in salt and sugar; add mustard seeds, dill, peppercorns, and habanero pepperflakes. Boil; stir until sugar and salt are dissolved.

Removed from heat; cool to room temperature, about 15 minutes.

Divide garlic and habanero peppers clove between 2 canning jars.

Divide avocado slices evenly between jars.

Stir vinegar mixture to evenly disburse seasoning; pour into jars.

Close the lids and place them in the refrigerator.

Chill until flavors combine, about 24 hours.

Nutrition: 106 kCal

Homemade Refrigerator Pickles

PreparationTime: 20 minutes
Cooking Time: 10 minutes
Servings: 64
Ingredients:

 1 cup distilled white vinegar
 1 tablespoon salt
 2 cups white sugar
 6 cups sliced cucumbers
 1 cup sliced onions
 1 cup sliced green bell peppers

Directions:
In a medium saucepan over medium heat, bring vinegar, salt, and sugar to a boil. Boil until the sugar has dissolved, about 10 minutes.
Place the onions, cucumbers, and greenbell peppers in a large bowl.
Pour the vinegar mixture over the vegetables.
Transfer to sterile containers and store them in the refrigerator.
Nutrition: 27 kCal

Quick Pickled Jalapeno Rings

PreparationTime: 5 minutes
Cooking Time: 20 minutes
Servings: 2
Ingredients:

 3/4 cupwater
 3/4 cup distilled whitevinegar
 3 tablespoons white sugar
 1 tablespoon koshersalt
 1 clove garlic, crushed
 1/2 teaspoonoregano
 10 large jalapeno peppers, sliced into rings

Directions:
Combine water, vinegar, sugar, kosher salt, garlic, and oregano in a saucepan over high heat.
Bring mixture to a boil, stir in jalapeno peppers and remove from heat.
Let mixture cool for 10 minutes.
Packpeppers into jars using tongs, cover with vinegar mixture, cover, and refrigerate until need. **Nutrition:** 99 kCal

Bread and ButterPickles II

PreparationTime: 1 hour
Cooking Time: 4 hours and 30 minutes
Servings: 50
Ingredients:

- 25 cucumbers, thinly sliced
- 6 onions, thinly sliced
- 2 green bell peppers, diced
- 3 cloves garlic, chopped
- ½ cup salt
- 3 cups cider vinegar
- 5 cups white sugar
- 2 tablespoons mustard seed
- 1 ½ teaspoons celery seed
- ½ teaspoon whole cloves
- 1 tablespoon ground turmeric

Directions:

In a large bowl, mix cucumbers, onions, greenbell peppers, garlic, and salt.

Allow standing approximately 3 hours.

Using a large saucepan, mix the cider vinegar, whitesugar, mustard seed, celery seed, whole cloves, and turmeric.

Bring to a boil.

Drain any liquid from the cucumber mixture.

Stir the cucumber mixture into the vinegar mixture.

Remove from heat shortly before the combined mixtures return to boil.

Transfer to sterile containers. Sealthen chill in the refrigerator until serving.

Nutrition: 105 kCal

Microwave Bread and Butter Pickles

Preparation Time:20 minutes
Cooking Time:10 minutes
Servings: 24
Ingredients:

　　1 large cucumber, sliced
　　1 teaspoon salt
　　1 onion, thinly sliced
　　½ teaspoon mustard seeds
　　1 cup white sugar
　　½ cup distilled white vinegar
　　¼ teaspoon celery seed
　　¼ ground turmeric

Directions:

In a mediummicrowave-safebowl, mix cucumber, salt, onion, mustard seeds, whitesugar, distilled whitevinegar, celery seed, and turmeric.

Microwave on high 7 to 8 minutes, stirring twice until cucumbers are tenderand onion is translucent. Transfer to sterile containers. Seal then chill in the refrigerator until serving.

Nutrition:36 kCal

Pickled Beets

Preparation Time: 30 minutes
Cooking Time: 20 minutes
Servings: 60
Ingredients:

- 10 pounds fresh smallbeets, stems removed
- 2 cups white sugar
- 1 tablespoon pickling salt
- 1 quart white vinegar
- 1/4 cup whole cloves

Directions:

Place beets in a big stockpot with a water to cover.

Bring to a boil, and cook until tender, about 15 minutes.

Cutthe large beets into quarters.

Drain, reserving 2 cups of the beetwater, cool and peel.

Sterilize jars and lids by immersing them in boiling water for at least 10 minutes.

Fill each jar with beets and add several whole cloves to each jar.

Using a large saucepan, combine the sugar, beetwater, vinegar, andpickling salt.

Bring to a rapid boil.

Pour the hot brine over the beets in the jars, andseal lids.

Place a rack in the bottom of a large stockpot then fill halfway with water.

Boil over high heat, then carefully lower the jars into the pot using a holder.

Leave a 2-inch space between the jars.

Pour in more boiling water until the water levelis at least 1 inch above the tops of the jars.

Boil the water, cover the pot, and process for 10 minutes.

Nutrition: 60 kCal

Hot ItalianGiardeniera
PreparationTime: 45 minutes
Cooking Time: 2 days and 2 hours
Servings: 10
Ingredients:

　　2 green bell peppers, diced
　　2 red bell peppers, diced8 fresh jalapeno peppers,
　　sliced 1 celery stalk, diced
　　1 medium carrot, diced
　　1 small onion, chopped
　　1/2 cup fresh cauliflower florets
　　1/2 cup saltwater to cover
　　2 cloves garlic, chopped
　　1 tablespoon dried oregano
　　1 teaspoon red pepperflakes
　　1/2 teaspoon blackpepper
　　1 (5 ounces) jar pimento-stuffed green olives, chopped
　　1 cup white vinegar
　　1 cupoliveoil

Directions:

Place in a bowl the jalapenos, green and redpeppers, celery, carrots, onion, and cauliflower. Stir in salt, and fill with enough cold water to cover.

Placeplastic wrap or aluminum foil over the bowl, and refrigerate overnight.

The next day, drain saltywater and rinse vegetables.

In a bowl, mix red pepper flakes, oregano, olives, black pepper, and garlic.

Pour and mix in vinegar and olive oil.

Combine with vegetable mixture, cover, andrefrigeratefor 2 days.

Nutrition: 233 kCal

CHAPTER 14:

Fermenting Recipes: Kefir

Vanilla Milk Kefir

Preparation Time: 5 minutes
Cooking Time: 0 minutes
Servings: 2 cups
Ingredients:
- 2 cups milk kefir.
- 1 to 2 teaspoons vanilla extract.

Directions:
Stir the vanilla extract into the milk kefir. Enjoy.
Nutrition: 72 kCal

Sweet Maple Kefir

Preparation Time: 5 minutes
Cooking Time: 0 minutes
Servings: 2 cups
Ingredients:
- 2 cups traditional milk kefir.
- Organic maple syrup

Directions:
Stir the maple syrup into the milk kefir. Taste it and add more syrup if it isn't sweet enough.
Nutrition: 130 kCal

Citrus Kefir

Preparation Time: 5 minutes
Cooking Time: 0 minutes
Servings: 2 cups
Ingredients:
- 2 cups milk kefir.
- 2 to 4 tablespoons citrus juice.

Directions:
Blend the citrus juice into the milk kefir and serve.
Nutrition: 67 kCal

Cocoa Spice Milk Kefir

Preparation Time: 10 minutes
Cooking Time: 12-48 hours
Servings: 4 cups
Ingredients:

> 4 cups milk kefir.
> 5 tablespoons cocoa powder.
> 2 cloves.
> 2 tablespoons ground cinnamon.
> ¼ tablespoon nutmeg.
> Organic cane sugar or stevia

Directions:

Make traditional milk kefir, letting the kefir ferment at room temperature for 24 hours.
Strain out the kefir grains and move them to fresh milk.
Add the cocoa powder, cloves, cinnamon and nutmeg and stir them into the kefir.
Place a lid on the kefir and let it ferment for an additional 12 to 24 hours.
Add sweetener and place an airtight lid on the container and move it to the fridge.
Nutrition: 94 kCal

Kefir Protein Power Shake

Preparation Time: 5 minutes
Cooking Time: 0 minutes
Servings: 2 cups
Ingredients:

> 1 ½ cups milk kefir.
> 1 – 2 scoops of your favorite protein powder blend.
> ½ cup milk.

Directions:

Place all of the ingredients in a big shaker bottle and shake until blended. Drink immediately.
Nutrition: 231 kCal

Rise and Shine Kefir

Preparation Time: 15 minutes
Cooking Time: 12-48 hours
Servings: 2 cups
Ingredients:
  - 2 cups milk kefir.
  - ½ cup carrot juice.
  - ½ cup shredded carrots.
  - 1 teaspoon vanilla extract.
  - Sweetener
  - Fermenting vessel.

Directions:
Make traditional milk kefir. The first ferment should last 12 to 24 hours. Strain out the kefir grains before adding any of the other ingredients to the fermenting vessel.

Place the milk kefir in the fermenting vessel and add the carrots, carrot juice and vanilla extract to the container.

Place the cover or lid on the container and allow it to ferment for an additional 12 to 24 hours. Move the container to the fridge until you're ready to consume the kefir.

Right before serving, place the kefir in the blender and blend everything together. Add sweetener. Stevia and rapadura are both good choices for sweeteners.

Nutrition: 270 kCal

Kefir Raspberry Flaxseed Fiber Booster

Preparation Time: 5 minutes
Cooking Time: 0 minutes
Servings: 2 cups
Ingredients:
  - 2 cups milk kefir.
  - 2 tablespoons ground flaxseed.
  - ½ cup raspberries.
  - Organic cane sugar (optional)

Directions:
Combine the ingredients mentioned above in a blender and blend them together. Add sweetener if you'd like. Serve.

Nutrition: 304 kCal

Sweet Lavender Milk Kefir
Preparation Time: 15 minutes
Cooking Time: 24-48 hours
Servings: 4 cups
Ingredients:
- 4 cups milk kefir.
- 2 tablespoons dried lavender flower heads.
- Organic cane sugar or stevia

Directions:
Make traditional milk kefir, letting the kefir ferment at room temperature for 24 hours.
Strain out the kefir grains and move them to fresh milk.
Stir the lavender flower heads into the milk kefir. Do not add the flower heads while the kefir grains are still in the kefir.
Place the lid on the kefir and let it sit at room temperature overnight. The second ferment should last 12 to 24 hours.
Strain the kefir to get rid of the flower heads.
Add cane sugar or stevia. Stir the sweetener into the kefir.
Place the kefir in an airtight container in the fridge.
Nutrition: 180 kCal

Sweet Raspberry Milk Kefir
Preparation Time: 5 minutes
Cooking Time: 0 minutes
Servings: 2 cups
Ingredients:
- 2 cups milk kefir.
- 3 tablespoons raspberry preserves (or more, if you'd like).
- Blender.

Directions:
Place the milk kefir and the raspberry preserves in the blender.
Blend them together.
Serve. You can blend ice into the kefir if you want it to be like a smoothie.
Nutrition: 140 kCal

Strawberry Banana Kefir Smoothie

Preparation Time: 5 minutes
Cooking Time: 0 minutes
Servings: 4 cups
Ingredients:

- 1 cup milk kefir.
- 6 to 8 strawberries.
- 1 banana.
- 5 ice cubes.

Directions:
Add the ingredients mentioned above to a blender and blend them together. Serve.
Nutrition: 140 kCal

Strawberry Lime Kefir Smoothie

Preparation Time: 5 minutes
Cooking Time: 0 minutes
Servings: 4 cups
Ingredients:

- 1 cup milk kefir.
- 2 tablespoons lime juice (or a whole lime).
- 5 strawberries.
- Organic cane sugar (optional)
- 5 ice cubes.

Directions:
The only step is to add all the ingredients mentioned above to a blender and blend it all together. Add sugar.
Nutrition: 178 kCal

Watermelon Slush Kefir Smoothie
Preparation Time: 5 minutes
Cooking Time: 0 minutes
Servings: 2 cups
Ingredients:
   1 cup milk kefir.
   2 cups seedless watermelon, chopped.
   10 ice cubes.
Directions:
Add the ingredients mentioned above to a blender and blend it all together. Serve.
Nutrition: 160 kCal

Piña Colada Kefir
Preparation Time: 5 minutes
Cooking Time: 0 minutes
Servings: 2 cups
Ingredients:
   1 cup milk kefir.
   ½ cup coconut cream.
   ½ cup pineapple juice.
   Blender.
Directions:
Place the milk kefir, coconut cream and pineapple juice in the blender.
Blend them together. Serve. You can blend ice into the kefir if you want it
to be like a smoothie. **Nutrition:** 130 kCal

Kefir Egg Nog
Preparation Time: 5 minutes
Cooking Time: 0 minutes
Servings: 4 cups
Ingredients:
   4 cups traditional kefir.
   2 eggs.
   2 to 3 tablespoons of organic cane
   sugar. ½ teaspoon cinnamon.
   ½ teaspoon nutmeg.
Directions:
Combine the kefir, eggs, sugar, cinnamon and nutmeg in a blender and pulse until smooth.
Sprinkle a bit of nutmeg mixed with cinnamon on top of each cup as you pour it.
Nutrition: 140 kCal

CHAPTER 15:

Dehydrating Recipes: Jerky and Some Extra

Beef Jerky
Preparation Time: 30 minutes
Cooking Time: 4 hours
Servings: 4
Ingredients:
- 2 lbs. London broil, sliced thinly
- 1 teaspoon sesame oil
- 3/4 teaspoon garlic powder
- 1 teaspoon onion powder
- 3 tablespoons Brown sugar
- 3 tablespoons Soy sauce

Directions:
Add all ingredients except meat in the large zip-lock bag and mix until well combined.
Add meat in a bag. Seal bag and massage gently to cover the meat with marinade.
Let marinate the meat for 30 minutes.
Arrange marinated meat slices in a single layer on the dehydrator racks and dehydrate at 160° F/ 71° C for 4 hours.
Nutrition: 347 kCal

Chicken Jerky

Preparation Time: 10 minutes
Cooking Time: 7 hours
Servings: 4
Ingredients:

    1 ½ lbs. chicken tenders, boneless, skinless and cut into ¼ inch strips
    ¼ teaspoon ground ginger
    ¼ teaspoon black pepper
    ½ teaspoon garlic powder
    1 teaspoon lemon juice
    ½ cup soy sauce

Directions:

Mix all ingredients except chicken into the zip-lock bag.

Add chicken and seal bag and mix until chicken is well coated. Place in refrigerator for 30 minutes.

Arrange marinated meat slices of dehydrator trays and dehydrate at 145° F/ 63°C for 6-7 hours.

Nutrition: 342 kCal

Ranch Beef Jerky

Preparation Time: 15 minutes
Cooking Time: 8 hours
Servings: 6
Ingredients:

    2 lbs. flank steak, cut into thin slices
    ¼ teaspoon cayenne pepper
    1 ½ teaspoons liquid smoke
    2 tablespoons red pepper flakes
    3 tablespoons ranch seasoning
    ¾ cup Worcestershire sauce
    ¾ cup soy sauce

Directions:

Add all ingredients and mix well. Cover bowl and place in the refrigerator overnight.

Arrange marinated meat slices on dehydrator racks and dehydrate at 145° F/ 63°C for 7-8 hours.

Nutrition: 346 kCal

Turkey Jerky

Preparation Time: 15 minutes
Cooking Time: 5 hours
Servings: 4
Ingredients:

- 1 lb. turkey meat, cut into thin slices
- 1 tsp. salt
- 2 teaspoons garlic powder
- 1 tablespoon onion powder
- 2 teaspoons brown sugar
- 1/3 cup Worcestershire sauce
- ¼ teaspoon Tabasco sauce
- 2 tablespoons soy sauce
- 1 tablespoon liquid smoke

Directions:

Add all ingredients except meat in the large zip-lock bag and mix until well combined.

Add meat in a bag. Seal bag and massage gently to cover the meat with marinade. Place in refrigerator for overnight.

Arrange marinated meat slices on the dehydrator racks and dehydrate at 160° F/ 71°C for 5 hours.

Nutrition: 233 kCal

Asian Pork Jerky

Preparation Time: 15 minutes
Cooking Time: 4 hours 30 minutes
Servings: 5
Ingredients:

- 1 lb. pork loin, cut into thin slices
- ¼ teaspoon salt
- 1 teaspoon black pepper
- ½ teaspoon onion powder
- ½ teaspoon garlic powder
- 1 teaspoon sesame oil
- 1 tablespoon chili garlic sauce
- 1 tablespoon brown sugar
- 1 tablespoon Worcestershire sauce
- 1/3 cup soy sauce

Directions:

Add all ingredients except meat slices into the large bowl and mix well.

Add sliced meat in the bowl and mix until well coated. Cover bowl and place inside the refrigerator overnight.

Arrange marinated meat slices on the dehydrator racks and dehydrate at 160° F/ 71°C for 4 1/2 hours.

Nutrition: 249 kCal

Tofu Jerky
Preparation Time: 10 minutes
Cooking Time: 4 hours
Servings: 4
Ingredients:
- 1 block tofu, pressed
- 4 drops liquid smoke
- 2 tablespoons Worcestershire sauce
- 2 tablespoons sriracha

Directions:
Cut tofu in half, then cut into the slices.
In a bowl, mix together liquid smoke, Worcestershire sauce, and sriracha.
Add tofu slices in a bowl and mix until well coated with the marinade. Cover bowl tightly and place in the refrigerator overnight.
Place marinated tofu slices on the dehydrator trays and dehydrate at 145° F/ 63° C for 4 hours.
Nutrition: 44 kCal

Sweet & Smoky Salmon Jerky
Preparation Time: 15 minutes
Cooking Time: 5 hours
Servings: 6
Ingredients:
- 2 lbs. salmon, sliced in strips
- 3 teaspoons black pepper
- 3 tablespoons smoked sea salt
- ¼ cup liquid smoke
- 2 tablespoons black pepper
- 1 cup brown sugar
- 1 cup soy sauce
- 1 orange juice

Directions:
Add all ingredients except salmon slices into the large bowl and mix well.
Add sliced salmon in the bowl and mix until well coated. Cover bowl and place inside the refrigerator overnight.
Arrange marinated salmon slices in a single layer on the dehydrator racks and dehydrate at 160° F/ 71°C for 5 hours.
Nutrition: 329 kCal

Lemon Salmon Jerky
Preparation Time: 15 minutes
Cooking Time: 4 hours
Servings: 6
Ingredients:
- 1 ¼ lbs. salmon, cut into ¼ inch slices
- 1/2 teaspoon liquid smoke
- 1 ¼ teaspoons black pepper
- 1 ½ tablespoons fresh lemon juice
- 1 tablespoon molasses
- ½ cup soy sauce, low sodium

Directions:
In a bowl, mix together liquid smoke, black pepper, lemon juice, molasses, and soy sauce.
Add sliced salmon into the bowl and mix until well coated. Cover bowl and place inside the refrigerator overnight.
Strain sliced salmon in colander and pat dry with a paper towel.
Arrange sliced salmon on a dehydrator tray and dehydrate at 145° F/ 63° C for 3-4 hours.
Nutrition: 148 kCal

Easy Mexican Jerky
Preparation Time: 15 minutes
Cooking Time: 5 hours
Servings: 4
Ingredients:
- 1 lb. pork lean meat, sliced thinly
- 1 teaspoon paprika
- ½ teaspoon oregano
- ½ teaspoon garlic powder
- 1 teaspoon chili powder
- ¼ teaspoon black pepper
- 1 teaspoon salt

Directions:
Add paprika, oregano, garlic powder, chili powder, black pepper, and salt in a bowl and mix well.
Add sliced meat in a bowl and mix until well coated. Cover the bowl and place inside the refrigerator overnight.
Arrange marinated meat slices on dehydrator rack and dehydrate at 160° F/ 71° C for 5 hours.
Nutrition:168 kCal

Perfect Lamb Jerky

Preparation Time: 10 minutes
Cooking Time: 6 hours
Servings: 6
Ingredients:

  2 ½ lbs. boneless lamb, trimmed fat and slice into thin strips
  ½ teaspoon black pepper
  1 tablespoon oregano
  1 teaspoon garlic powder
  1 ½ teaspoons onion powder
  3 tablespoons Worcestershire sauce
  1/3 cup soy sauce

Directions:
Add soy sauce, Worcestershire sauce, onion powder, garlic powder, oregano, and black pepper in the large bowl and mix well.
Add meat slices in the bowl and mix until well coated. Cover bowl tightly and place in the refrigerator overnight.
Arrange marinated meat slices on dehydrator racks and dehydrate to 145° F/ 63° C for 5-6 hours.
Nutrition: 373 kCal

Dehydrated Yogurt

Preparation Time: 30 minutes
Cooking Time: 24 hours
Servings: 3
Ingredients:

  1 gallon milk
  1 quart cream
  Yogurt starter

Directions:
Put a deep pot over heat and pour the milk in it. Stir it occasionally with a gap of about 10 minutes until it comes to a boil.
Remove from heat and cover the pot. Allow the milk to chill to a temperature where you can comfortably touch it. Then add the yogurt starter and stir.
Pour the milk and starter mixture into glass containers and place them in the dehydrator at 100° for 24 hours. After this much time, the yogurt will be ready. Store it in the fridge for a few hours and then enjoy!
Nutrition: 100 kCal

CHAPTER 16:

Dehydrating Recipes: Powder, Spices, Etc.

Homemade Chili Powder
Preparation Time: 10 minutes
Cooking Time: 6 hours 15 minutes
Servings: 24
Ingredients:
    12 red chili peppers
Directions:
Place Parallax Screens on the racks of your Excalibur Food Dehydrator. Carefully slice the chili peppers into thin strips. Note: The amount of heat in your chili powder will depend on how much pith and seed you allow to stay with the peppers. If you want super-hot powder to keep the seeds and pith. For less spicy powder discard most of the seeds and pith.
Lay the peppers (and seeds and pith if desired) on the screens and set your Excalibur to 115F. Dehydrate for about 5 to 6 hours or until the peppers are dried. Transfer the contents of your Excalibur to a blender and pulse until a rough powder form. Store in jars or zipper lock bags.
Nutrition: 24 kCal

Spicy Carrot Powder

Preparation Time: 15 minutes
Cooking Time: 6 hours 15 minutes
Servings: 12
Ingredients:

   6 large carrots, peeled, chopped
   2 jalapeño peppers, sliced
   1 tablespoon salt

Directions:

Place the carrots in a food processor. Pulse until the carrots are roughly chopped but not a puree.
Place Parallax Screens on the racks of your Excalibur Food Dehydrator and use all but one rack for the carrots. Make sure the carrots are in thin even layers not thicker than 1/4 inch.
Use one rack for the jalapeño peppers. Set your Excalibur to 150F and dehydrate for 6 hours or until the carrots are dry.
Transfer the dried carrots and jalapeños to a blender and blend until you get a fine powder. Store in jars or zipper lock bags.
Nutrition:40 kCal

Tasty Pineapple Chunks

Preparation Time: 10 minutes
Cooking Time: 12 hours
Servings: 4
Ingredients:

   1 ripe pineapple

Directions:

Peel and cut pineapple. Cut in half and then cut in ¼ inch thick chunks.

Place pineapple chunks on dehydrator racks and dehydrate at 135 F/ 58 C for 12 hours.

Nutrition: 62 kCal

Dried Mango

Preparation Time: 5 Minutes
Cooking Time: 8 Hours
Servings: 2
Ingredients:

   ½ mango, peeled, pitted, and cut into ⅜-inch slices

Directions:

Arrange the mango slices flat in a single layer in the Cook & Crisp Basket. Place in the pot and close the Crisping Lid.

Press Dehydrate, set the temperature to 135°F, and set the time to 8 hours. Select Start/Stop to begin.

When dehydrating is complete, remove the basket from the pot and transfer the mango slices to an airtight container.

Nutrition: 67 kCal

Simple Apple Leather
Preparation Time: 5 minutes
Cooking Time: 6 hours
Servings: 12
Ingredients:
   8 cups applesauce
   1 3oz. box sugar free jello
Directions:
In a large bowl, combine both the apple sauce and Jello. Place ParaFlexx Screens on the racks of your Excalibur and pour the puree onto the screens. Use a spatula to spread the puree about 1/8 inch thick evenly.
Set your Excalibur to 140F and dehydrate for 6 hours. Make sure the leather is dehydrated and not sticky before removing it from the screens.
Nutrition:103 kCal

Mirepoix Powder
Preparation Time: 20 minutes
Cooking Time: 6 hours
Servings: 24
Ingredients:
   2 yellow onions, thinly sliced
   3 carrots, sliced into thin rounds
   3 stalks celery, cut into thin slices
Directions:
Place ParaFlexx Screens on the racks of your Excalibur Food Dehydrator. On separate racks place layers of onion, carrot, and celery. Make sure they are even layers.
Set your Excalibur to 150F and dehydrate for 6 hours.
When the vegetables are dehydrated, place them in a blender together. Blend until a fine powder form. Store the powder in jars and use it as the base for many soups and sauces.
Nutrition:7 kCal

Int Leaves
Preparation Time: 10 minutes
Cooking Time: 6 hours 10 minutes
Servings: 12
Ingredients:
  2 bunches of fresh peppermint
Directions:
The leaves on the rack of your Excalibur Food Dehydrator and set to 150F. Dehydrate for 6 hours.
Remove mint leaves from the racks and store them in jars or zipper lock bags until ready to use.
Nutrition: 96 kCal

Dried Rose Petals
Preparation Time: 10 minutes
Cooking Time: 4 to 5 hours
Servings: 15
Ingredients:
  Fresh rose petals, stems removed
Directions:
Select the type of rose you would like to use. Different varieties have different aromas, and some are stronger and sweeter than others.
For best results, only dehydrate one type of flower at a time because different types of roses require different drying times.
Remove the stems of the rose petals and place the petals on the rack of your Excalibur Food Dehydrator in single layers.
Set your Excalibur to 115F and dehydrate for 4 to 5 hours, or until the petals are dehydrated.
Your dried rose petals should retain their intense aromas for several months.
Nutrition: 37 kCal

Pumpkin Chips
Preparation Time: 15 minutes
Cooking Time: 18 hours 10 minutes
Servings: 6
Ingredients:
   1 pumpkin
   2 tablespoons coconut oil, melted
   1 teaspoon cinnamon
   1 teaspoon nutmeg
Directions:
Remove the seeds, pulp, and skin from the pumpkin, and slice the pumpkin flesh into thin slices. Try to make the slices no more than 1/8 inch thick.

In a large bowl, combine the pumpkin slices, coconut oil, cinnamon, nutmeg, and salt. Stir well to coat.

Place the pumpkin slices on the racks of your Excalibur and set them to 125F. Dehydrated for 18 hours or until the slices are crispy.
Nutrition: 140 kCal

Citrus Potpourri
Preparation Time: 20 minutes
Cooking Time: 12 hours 15 minutes
Servings: 5
Ingredients:
   2 lemons
   2 oranges
   6 cinnamon sticks
   3 tablespoons dried cloves
Directions:
Slice the lemons and oranges between 1/8 and 1/4-inch-thick and place them on the racks of your Excalibur Food Dehydrator in a single layer so the slices are not touching.

Set your Excalibur to 150F and dehydrate for 12 hours. The citrus should be dry and firm to the touch and not sticky.

Remove the slices from the racks and divide among bowls or jars with equal amounts of cinnamon sticks and dried cloves.
Nutrition: 190 kCal

Crunch Green Bean Chips

Preparation Time: 15 minutes
Cooking Time: 12 hours 10 minutes
Servings: 12
Ingredients:

- 3 lbs. Fresh green beans
- 1/4 cup coconut oil, melted
- 1 tablespoon salt

Directions:

Combine your green beans and oil and mix well to cover. Season with salt and mix once more. Put the green beans on the racks of your Excalibur and set them to 125F. Dehydrate the beans for 12 hours or until the beans are dried out and firm.

Remove the green beans from the dehydrator and keep them in a cool dry spot.

Nutrition: 130 kCal

Chia Seed Pudding

Preparation Time: 10 minutes **Cooking Time:** 0 minutes **Servings:** 3
Ingredients:

- 2 cups of unsweetened almond milk 1 tablespoon of raw honey
- ½ cup of chia seeds
- ½ cup fresh blueberries

Directions:

Using a large bowl, stir the chia seeds, almond milk, maple syrup, and vanilla extract. Refrigerate for at least 3-4 hours, stirring occasionally. Serve with the topping of strawberry slices. **Nutrition:** 139 kCal

Dried Cilantro
Preparation Time: 10 minutes
Cooking Time: 3 hours 10 minutes
Servings: 12
Ingredients:
   2 bunches of fresh cilantro
Directions:
You can dehydrate your cilantro with or without the stems; it's totally up to you. Rinse and dry the cilantro and place it in a single layer on the racks of your Excalibur Food Dehydrator.
Set your Excalibur to 110F and dehydrate for 3 hours. Remove the dried cilantro from the racks and store in jars or zipper lock bags until ready to use.
Nutrition: 3.68 kCal

Tomato Powder
Preparation Time: 10 minutes
Cooking Time: 4 hours 10 minutes
Servings: 24
Ingredients:
   3 lbs. fresh tomatoes
Directions:
Slice the tomatoes about a 1/8 inch thick. Place ParaFlexx Screens on the racks of your Excalibur Food Dehydrator.
Lay the tomato slices on the screens in a single layer so they do not touch. Set your Excalibur Food Dehydrator to 150F and dehydrate for 4 hours.
When tomatoes are entirely dehydrated, transfer them to a blender, and pulse until a fine powder form. Store the powder in a jar or zipper lock bag.
Nutrition: 86 kCal

Plum Fruit Leather

Preparation Time: 30 minutes
Cooking Time: 8 hours 20 minutes
Servings: 12
Ingredients:
- 6 purple or red plums split and pitted
- 2 tablespoons lemon juice
- 2 teaspoons ground cinnamon
- 1/4 cup water

Directions:
Place the plums and water in a pot and simmer until the plums begin to break down, about 10 to 15 minutes.

When the plums are soft, pour into a blender and blend until smooth. Add the lemon juice and cinnamon and blend.

Place ParaFlexx Screens on the racks of your Excalibur and set them to 140F.

Pour the puree onto the screens and use a spatula to spread the puree evenly, about 1/8 inch thick.

Dehydrate for 8 hours. Make sure the leather is entirely dehydrated and not sticky before removing it from the screens.

Nutrition: 31 kCal

CHAPTER 17:

Dehydrating Recipes using Air Fryer

Eggplant Jerky
Preparation Time: 10 minutes
Cooking Time: 12 hours
Servings: 4
Ingredients:
- 1 eggplant, sliced
- 1 tsp. paprika
- 1/2 tsp. black pepper
- 1 garlic clove, minced
- 1/2 cup vinegar
- 1/2 cup olive oil
- 1/2 tsp. sea salt

Directions:
Add eggplant slices into the large bowl.
Add remaining ingredients and toss well. Cover and set aside for 2 hours.
Place the dehydrating tray in a multi-level air fryer basket and place the basket in the instant pot.
Arrange marinated eggplant slices on dehydrating tray.
Seal pot with air fryer lid and select dehydrate mode then set temperature to 115 F and timer for 12 hours.
Nutrition:254 kCal

Dehydrated Pear Slices

Preparation Time: 10 minutes
Cooking Time: 5 hours
Servings: 3
Ingredients:

- 2 pears, cut into 1/4-inch thick slices
- 1 tbsp lemon juice

Directions:

In a big bowl, mix lemon juice and 2 cups of water.

Add pear slices into the lemon water and soak for 10 minutes.

Place the dehydrating tray in a multi-level air fryer basket and place the basket in the instant pot.

Place pear slices on the dehydrating tray.

Seal pot with air fryer lid and select dehydrate mode then set temperature to 160 F and timer for 5 hours.

Nutrition: 82 kCal

Delicious Nacho Zucchini Chips

Preparation Time: 10 minutes
Cooking Time: 6 hours
Servings: 2
Ingredients:

- 1 yellow squash, sliced thinly
- 1/2 tsp. tomato powder
- 1/4 tsp. paprika
- 1/2 tsp. chili powder
- 1/4 tsp. onion powder
- 1/4 tsp. garlic powder
- 1 tbsp cheddar cheese, grated
- Salt

Directions:

Add squash slices into the mixing bowl. Add remaining ingredients and toss well.

Place the dehydrating tray in a multi-level air fryer basket and place the basket in the instant pot.

Arrange squash slices on the dehydrating tray.

Seal pot with air fryer lid and select dehydrate mode then set temperature to 135 F and timer for 6 hours.

Nutrition: 110 kCal

Apple Sweet Potato Fruit Leather
Preparation Time: 10 minutes
Cooking Time: 4 hours
Servings: 2
Ingredients:
   1/2 cup mashed sweet potatoes
   1/4 tsp. cinnamon
   1 tbsp honey
   1/2 cup applesauce
Directions:
Firstly, add all said ingredients into the blender and blend until smooth.
Place the dehydrating tray in a multi-level air fryer basket and place the basket in the instant pot.
Line dehydrating tray with parchment paper.
Spread blended mixture on dehydrating tray.
Seal pot with air fryer lid and select dehydrate mode then set temperature to 110 F and timer for 4 hours or until leathery.
Nutrition: 123 kCal

Corn Chips
Preparation Time: 10 minutes
Cooking Time: 8 hours
Servings: 2
Ingredients:
   1 cup sweet corn
   Pepper
   Salt
Directions:
Add corn, pepper, and salt into the blender and blend until creamy.
Place the dehydrating tray in a multi-level air fryer basket and place the basket in the instant pot.
Line dehydrating tray with parchment paper.
Spread corn mixture on dehydrating tray.
Seal pot with air fryer lid and select dehydrate mode then set temperature to 115 F and timer for 8 hours.
Nutrition: 66 kCal

CANNING AND PRESERVING FOR BEGINNERS:

Strawberry Mango Fruit Leather

Preparation Time: 10 minutes
Cooking Time: 4 hours
Servings: 2
Ingredients:
- 1/4 cup fresh strawberries
- 1/2 mango, peel and chopped

Directions:
Add strawberries and mango into the blender and blend until smooth.
Place the dehydrating tray in a multi-level air fryer basket and place the basket in the instant pot.
Line dehydrating tray with parchment paper.
Spread blended fruit mixture on dehydrating tray.
Seal pot with air fryer lid and select dehydrate mode then set temperature to 160 F and timer for 4 hours.
Nutrition: 56 kCal

Banana Chocolate Fruit Leather

Preparation Time: 10 minutes
Cooking Time: 10 hours
Servings: 2
Ingredients:
- 1 banana
- 1/4 tbsp brown sugar
- 1/2 tbsp cocoa powder

Directions:
Add banana, brown sugar, and cocoa powder into the blender and blend until smooth.
Place the dehydrating tray in a multi-level air fryer basket and place the basket in the instant pot.
Line dehydrating tray with parchment paper.
Spread banana mixture on dehydrating tray.
Seal pot with air fryer lid and select dehydrate mode then set temperature to 130 F and timer for 10 hours.
Nutrition: 60 kCal

Spicy Chickpeas

Preparation Time: 10 minutes
Cooking Time: 10 hours
Servings: 2
Ingredients:

- 10 oz. can chickpeas, drained and rinsed
- 1/2 tbsp sugar
- 1 1/2 tbsp sriracha
- Salt

Directions:

In a bowl, mix together chickpeas, sugar, sriracha, and salt.

Place the dehydrating tray in a multi-level air fryer basket and place the basket in the instant pot. Arrange chickpeas on dehydrating tray.

Seal pot with air fryer lid and select dehydrate mode then set temperature to 130 F and timer for 10 hours.

Nutrition: 191 kCal

Pumpkin Fruit Leather

Preparation Time: 10 minutes
Cooking Time: 8 hours
Servings: 2
Ingredients:

- 1/2 cup pumpkin puree
- 1/8 tsp. ground allspice
- 1/8 tsp. ground nutmeg
- 1/4 tsp. cinnamon
- 1 tbsp shredded coconut
- 1 tbsp honey
- 1/2 cup applesauce
- 1/4 cup coconut milk

Directions:

Place the dehydrating tray in a multi-level air fryer basket and place the basket in the instant pot. Line dehydrating tray with parchment paper.

Add all said ingredients into the bowl and mix until well combined and spread mixture on dehydrating tray.

Seal pot with air fryer lid and select dehydrate mode then set temperature to 135 F and timer for 8 hours.

Nutrition: 159 kCal

Dried Lemon Slices

Preparation Time: 10 minutes
Cooking Time: 10 hours
Servings: 4
Ingredients:

2 lemons, wash and cut into 1/4-inch thick slices

Directions:

Place the dehydrating tray in a multi-level air fryer basket and place the basket in the instant pot. Arrange lemon slices on dehydrating tray.

Seal pot with air fryer lid and select dehydrate mode then set temperature to 125 F and timer for 10 hours.

Nutrition: 8 kCal

Parsnips Chips

Preparation Time: 10 minutes
Cooking Time: 6 hours
Servings: 2
Ingredients:

1 parsnip, cut into 1/4-inch thick slices
Pepper
Salt

Directions:

Add parsnip slices, pepper, and salt into the bowl and toss well.

Place the dehydrating tray in a multi-level air fryer basket and place the basket in the instant pot. Arrange parsnip slices on dehydrating tray.

Seal pot with air fryer lid and select dehydrate mode then set temperature to 125 F and timer for 6 hours.

Nutrition: 50 kCal

Cauliflower Popcorn

Preparation Time: 10 minutes
Cooking Time: 8 hours
Servings: 2
Ingredients:

2 cups cauliflower florets, chopped
1/4 tsp. ground cumin
1/2 tsp. cayenne
1/2 tbsp paprika
2 tbsp hot sauce
1 1/2 tbsp olive oil

Directions:

Add cauliflower into the large bowl.

Add remaining ingredients over the cauliflower and toss well.

Place the dehydrating tray in a multi-level air fryer basket and place the basket in the instant pot.

Place cauliflower pieces on dehydrating tray.

Seal pot with air fryer lid and select dehydrate mode then set temperature to 130 F and timer for 8 hours.

Nutrition: 124 kCal

Dehydrated Okra

Preparation Time: 10 minutes
Cooking Time: 24 hours
Servings: 2
Ingredients:

6 pods okra, slice into rounds

Directions:

Place the dehydrating tray in a multi-level air fryer basket and place the basket in the instant pot.

Arrange sliced okra on dehydrating tray.

Seal pot with air fryer lid and select dehydrate mode then set temperature to 130 F and timer for 24 hours.

Nutrition:26 kCal

Cucumber Chips
Preparation Time: 10 minutes
Cooking Time: 10 hours
Servings: 2
Ingredients:
    1 cucumber, sliced thinly
    1 tsp. apple cider vinegar
    1/2 tbsp olive oil
    Salt
Directions:
Toss cucumber slices with vinegar, oil, and salt.
Place the dehydrating tray in a multi-level air fryer basket and place the basket in the instant pot.
Arrange cucumber slices on dehydrating tray.
Seal pot with air fryer lid and select dehydrate mode then set temperature to 135 F and timer for 10 hours.
Nutrition:53 kCal

CHAPTER 18:

Dehydrating Recipes: Chips and Snacks

Zucchini Chips
Preparation Time: 15 minutes
Cooking Time: 12 hours
Servings: 8
Ingredients:

      4 cups zucchini, sliced thinly
      2 tbsp. balsamic vinegar
      2 tbsp. olive oil
      2 tsp. sea salt

Directions:
Add olive oil, balsamic vinegar, and also sea salt to the large bowl and stir well.
Add sliced zucchini into the bowl and toss well.
Arrange the zucchini slices on dehydrator trays and dehydrate at 135 F/ 58 C for 8-12 hours.
Store in an air-tight container.
Nutrition:40 kCal

Brussels Sprout Chips

Preparation Time: 15 minutes
Cooking Time: 10 hours
Servings: 6
Ingredients:

> 2 lbs. Brussels sprouts, wash, dry, cut the root and separate leaves
> 2 fresh lemon juice
> ½ cup water
> ¼ cup nutritional yeast
> 1 jalapeno pepper halved and remove seeds
> 1 cup cashews
> 2 bell peppers
> 1 tsp. sea salt

Directions:

Add Brussels sprouts leaves to the large bowl and set aside.

Add bell peppers, water, lemon juice, nutritional yeast, jalapeno, cashews, and salt to the blender and blend until smooth.

Pour blended mixture over Brussels sprouts leaves and toss until well coated.

Arrange Brussels sprouts on dehydrator trays and dehydrate at 125 F/ 52 C for 10 hours.

Allow to cool. After which, store in an air-tight container.

Nutrition: 237 kCal

Eggplant Slices

Preparation Time: 10 minutes
Cooking Time: 4 hours
Servings: 4
Ingredients:

> 1 medium eggplant, cut into ¼ inch thick slices
> ¼ tsp. onion powder
> ¼ tsp. garlic powder
> 1 ½ tsp. paprika

Directions:

Add theall ingredients into the mixing bowl and toss well.

Arrange eggplant slices on dehydrator trays and dehydrate at 145 F/ 63 C for 4 hours or until crispy.

Store in an air-tight container.

Nutrition: 32 kCal

Kale Chips
Preparation Time: 10 minutes
Cooking Time: 4 hours
Servings: 4
Ingredients:

>   2 kale heads
>   1 tsp. garlic powder
>   1 tsp. sea salt
>   1 tbsp. fresh lemon juice
>   3 tbsp. nutritional yeast
>   2 tbsp. olive oil

Directions:
Wash kale and cut into bits.
Add the left over ingredients into the bowl and mix well.
Add kale bits to the bowl and mix until well coated.
Arrange kale bits on dehydrator trays and dehydrate at 145 F/ 63 C for 3-4 hours or until crispy.
Nutrition:111 kCal

Dried Bell Peppers
Preparation Time: 10 minutes
Cooking Time: 24 hours
Servings: 4
Ingredients:

>   4 bell peppers cut in half and de-seed

Directions:
Cut bell peppers in strips then cut each strip into ½ inch pieces.
Arrange bell peppers strips on dehydrator racks and dehydrate at 135 F/ 58 C for 12-24 hours or until crisp.
Store in an air-tight container.
Nutrition:38kCal

Avocado Chips
Preparation Time: 15 minutes
Cooking Time: 10 hours
Servings: 4
Ingredients:
>4 avocados, halved and pitted
>¼ tsp. sea salt
>¼ tsp. cayenne pepper
>¼ cup fresh cilantro, chopped
>½ lemon juice

Directions:
Cut avocado into the slices.
Drizzle lemon juice over avocado slices.
Arrange avocado slices on dehydrator trays and sprinkle with cayenne pepper, salt and cilantro dehydrate at 160 F/ 71 C for 10 hours.
Nutrition:62 kCal

Sweet Potato Chips
Preparation Time: 10 minutes
Cooking Time: 12 hours
Servings: 2
Ingredients:
>2 sweet potatoes peel and sliced thinly
>1/8 tsp. ground cinnamon
>1 tsp. coconut oil, melted
>Seal salt

Directions:
Add sweet potato slices into a bowl. Add cinnamon, coconut oil, and salt and toss well.
Arrange sweet potato slices on dehydrator trays and dehydrate at 125 F/ 52 C for 12 hours.
Store in an air-tight container.
Nutrition:132 kCal

Healthy Squash Chips

Preparation Time: 10 minutes
Cooking Time: 12 hours
Servings: 8
Ingredients:

> 1 yellow squash, cut into 1/8 inch thick slices
> 2 tbsp. apple cider vinegar
> 2 tsp. olive oil
> Salt

Directions:

Add all the necessary ingredients into the bowl and toss well.

Arrange squash slices on dehydrator trays and dehydrate at 115 F/ 46 C for 12 hours or until crispy.

Store in an air-tight container.

Nutrition: 15 kCal

Broccoli Chips

Preparation Time: 15 minutes
Cooking Time: 12 hours
Servings: 4
Ingredients:

> 1 lb. broccoli, cut into florets 1
> tsp. onion powder
> 1 garlic clove
> ½ cup vegetable broth
> ¼ cup hemp seeds
> 2 tbsp. nutritional yeast

Directions:

Add broccoli florets into a large mixing bowl and set aside.

Add remaining ingredients into the blender and blend until smooth.

Pour blended mixture over broccoli florets and toss well.

Arrange broccoli florets on dehydrator trays and dehydrate at 115 F/ 46 C for 10-12 hours.

Nutrition: 106 kCal

Fruit Lollipops

Preparation Time: 15 minutes
Cooking Time: 15 hours
Servings: 3-4
Ingredients:

> Kiwi, bananas, apples
> 1 tbsp. caster sugar juice
> Water
> Lemon juice

Directions:
Peel and cut the fruit into slices of about 5 mm then put them in the dryer at 235°F until dehydrated. On a sheet of parchment paper lay the dried slices slightly sticking the toothpick into the pulp and pour over the dissolved sugar with water and lemon. Let it solidify for 15 minutes then put the lollipops in the dryer at 113°F for an hour.
Nutrition:11 kCal

CHAPTER 19:

Appendix: Measurement Conversion Table

Volume Equivalents (Liquid)

US STANDARD	US STANDARD (OUNCES)	METRIC (APPROXIMATE)
2 tablespoons	1 fl. oz.	30 mL
¼ cup	2 fl. oz.	60 mL
½ cup	4 fl. oz.	120 mL
1 cup	8 fl. oz.	240 mL
1½ cups	12 fl. oz.	355 mL
2 cups or 1 pint	16 fl. oz.	475 mL
4 cups or 1 quart	32 fl. oz.	1 L
1 gallon	128 fl. oz.	4 L

Volume Equivalents (Dry)

US STANDARD	METRIC (APPROXIMATE)
⅛ teaspoon	0.5 mL
¼ teaspoon	1 mL
½ teaspoon	2 mL
¾ teaspoon	4 mL
1 teaspoon	5 mL
1 tablespoon	15 mL
¼ cup	59 mL
⅓ cup	79 mL
½ cup	118 mL
⅔ cup	156 mL
¾ cup	177 mL
1 cup	235 mL
2 cups or 1 pint	475 mL
3 cups	700 mL
4 cups or 1 quart	1 L

Oven Temperatures

FAHRENHEIT (F)	CELSIUS (C) (APPROXIMATE)
250°	120°
300°	150°
325°	165°
350°	180°
375°	190°
400°	200°
425°	220°
450°	230°

Weight Equivalent

US STANDARD	METRIC (APPROXIMATE)
½ ounce	15 g
1 ounce	30 g
2 ounces	60 g
4 ounces	115 g
8 ounces	225 g
12 ounces	340 g
16 ounces or 1 pound	455 g

Conclusion

T here are numerous valid reasons for preserving and canning at home. Starting canning and preserving foods could really help you save more and provide you with various choices.

When you take the time to really sit down and think about it, having a practical understanding of how to preserve and put up the bunt of the summer is critical to finding success in the homesteading lifestyle. You shouldn't look at this book as the be-all, end-all of food preservation. This is just the tip of the iceberg.

Once you get a handleon the basic techniques you can start expanding and branching out into all kinds of other creative endeavors. Thefirsthalfdozenor so timesthrough, just try to remember to keep it simple. Always remember thatwhether you are puttingthings up in the root cellar, pickling, fermentingor canning thatsterilization is the most important key to success. Five more minutesofextra effort could make the difference between dumping a case of jars into the compost pile and a pantry full of summer's flavorful goodies.

Once you are the grandmaestro of sterilization and you've got a bunchof successful batchesput up for the season, then you can startplayingwith your own creative ideas. By waitinguntil the bumper crop to get creative, you ensure that you've got enough to put up already to get you through the leanwinternights.

When you do start to strikeoutwith your owncreativeadditions try to keep it to one or two newingredients. Sometimes, there are some that seems like a greatidea in your mindthat can muddle the flavors or over power the flavorof the original fruit, vegetable or meat. Being able to know just which addition is the culprit is a loteasier when you're only dealingwith one or two possible suspects. Also doesn't forget about the importance ofshelvingspace. In 2007 I got over zealous withmycanning. Before you knewit I wastearingapart old pallets for the lumber to line my oldbasement stairwell with shelves. Of course this lead to couple hundredsplinters, which lead me to a weekend ofsanding and painting. Sure, in the end Iprobably saved $20 or $30, but if I wouldhaveponied up a few more dollars I could havejustbought some garage shelvesaheadof time that wererated to hand 250 poundspershelf. Thelesson of the story is that before you get too excited about putting up a couple hundredcansoffruits and veggies, you reallywant to look around and understand the space you have available.

Enjoy the process of preserving your bounty and remember to followsafe practices when preserving your food, especially when canning. If you have any doubt, confusion orquestions about safe procedures or methods, refer to this book whenever you need to and followthe information you findhere. This book is made for your queries and questions in mind.

Made in United States
Troutdale, OR
02/18/2024